Aliza Garrison

LITERATURE CONNECTIONS

The Tragedy of Romeo and Juliet

and Related Readings

 McDougal Littell
A HOUGHTON MIFFLIN COMPANY

Evanston, IL Dallas Phoenix Columbia, SC

Acknowledgments

John Hawkins & Associates, Inc.: Excerpt from *Twisted Tales from Shakespeare* by Richard Armour; Copyright 1957. Reprinted by permission of John Hawkins & Associates, Inc.

Harry Mark Petrakis: "The Wooing of Ariadne" from *Collected Stories* by Harry Mark Petrakis, Lake View Press, Chicago, Illinois. Copyright © 1987 by Harry Mark Petrakis.

Random House Inc.: Excerpt from *A Natural History of Love* by Diane Ackerman; Copyright © 1994 by Diane Ackerman. Reprinted by permission of Random House Inc.

WGBH TV: "Romeo and Juliet in Sarajevo" written and directed by John Zaritsky, from *Frontline*, aired May 10, 1994. Reprinted by permission of WGBH TV, Boston, and *Frontline*.

The editors have made every effort to trace the ownership of all copyrighted selections found in this book and to make full acknowledgment for their use. Omissions brought to our attention will be corrected in a subsequent edition.

Cover illustration by Curtis Parker.
Author photo: North Wind Picture Archive.

ISBN 0-395-77537-X

8 9 10 11 12 13 14 15 – DCI –03 02 01 00 99

Contents

Continued

The Tragedy of Romeo and Juliet

William Shakespeare

Cast of Characters

THE MONTAGUES

Lord Montague (män' tə gyo͞o')

Lady Montague

Romeo, son of Montague

Benvolio (ben vō' lē ō), nephew of Montague and friend of Romeo

Balthasar (bäl' thə sär'), servant to Romeo

Abram, servant to Montague

THE CAPULETS

Lord Capulet (kap' yo͞o let')

Lady Capulet

Juliet, daughter of Capulet

Tybalt (ti' bält), nephew of Lady Capulet

Nurse to Juliet

Peter, servant to Juliet's Nurse

Sampson
Gregory } servants to Capulet

An old man of the Capulet family

Continued

OTHERS

Prince Escalus (es' kə lus), ruler of Verona

Mercutio (mər kyōō' shē ō'), kinsman of the
   Prince and friend of Romeo

Friar Laurence, a Franciscan priest

Friar John, another Franciscan priest

Count Paris, a young nobleman, kinsman of the Prince

Apothecary (ə päth' ə ker' ē)

Page to Paris

Chief Watchman

Three Musicians

An Officer

**Citizens of Verona, Gentlemen and Gentlewomen of
   both houses, Maskers, Torchbearers, Pages, Guards,
   Watchmen, Servants, and Attendants.**

Time: The fourteenth century

Place: Verona (və rō' nə); Mantua (man' chōō wə) in
   northern Italy

3-4 *ancient . . . unclean:* A new outbreak of fighting *(mutiny)* between families has caused the citizens of Verona to have one another's blood on their hands.

6 *star-crossed:* doomed. The position of the stars when the lovers were born was not favorable. In Shakespeare's day, people took astrology and horoscopes very seriously.

11 *but:* except for; *naught:* nothing.

12 *two hours' . . . stage:* the action that will take place on the stage during the next two hours.

14 *What . . . mend:* We will fill in the details that have been left out of the prologue.

THE PROLOGUE

The CHORUS is one actor who serves as a narrator. He enters from the back of the stage to introduce and explain the theme of the play. His job is to "hook" the audience's interest by telling them just enough to quiet them down and make them eager for more. In this prologue, or preview, the narrator explains that the play will be about a feud between two families (the Capulets and the Montagues). In addition, the narrator says that the feud will end in tragedy. As you read the prologue, determine what the tragedy will be.

[Enter Chorus.]

Chorus. Two households, both alike in dignity,
In fair Verona, where we lay our scene,
From ancient grudge break to new mutiny,
Where civil blood makes civil hands unclean.
5   From forth the fatal loins of these two foes,
A pair of star-crossed lovers take their life,
Whose misadventured piteous overthrows
Doth with their death bury their parents' strife.
The fearful passage of their death-marked love,
10   And the continuance of their parents' rage,
Which, but their children's end, naught could remove,
Is now the two hours' traffic of our stage,
The which if you with patient ears attend,
What here shall miss, our toil shall strive to mend.

[Exit.]

1-5 ***we'll not carry coals:*** We won't stand to be insulted. (Those involved in the dirty work of hauling coal were often the targets of jokes and insults.) Here the comic characters Gregory and Sampson are bragging about how brave they are. Their boasts include several bad jokes based on words that sound alike: ***collier*** means "coal dealer"; ***in choler*** means "angry"; ***collar*** refers to a hangman's noose.

ACT ONE

Scene 1 *A public square in Verona.*

As the scene opens, two young Capulet servants swagger across the stage joking and bragging. When they happen to meet servants from the rival house of Montague, a quarrel begins that grows into an ugly street fight. Finally the ruler of Verona, Prince Escalus, appears. He is angry about the violence in his city and warns that the next offenders will receive the death penalty. The crowd fades away and the stage is set for the entrance of Romeo, heir of the Montague family. Romeo, lovesick and miserable, can talk of nothing but his love for Rosaline and her cruelty in refusing to love him back.

[Enter Sampson and Gregory, servants of the house of Capulet, armed with swords and bucklers (shields).]

Sampson. Gregory, on my word, we'll not carry coals.

Gregory. No, for then we should be colliers.

Sampson. I mean, an we be in choler, we'll draw.

Gregory. Ay, while you live, draw your neck out of
5   collar.

Sampson. I strike quickly, being moved.

Gregory. But thou art not quickly moved to strike.

Sampson. A dog of the house of Montague moves me.

Gregory. To move is to stir, and to be valiant is
10   to stand. Therefore, if thou art moved, thou
    runnest away.

13 *take the wall:* walk nearest to the wall. People of higher rank had the privilege of walking closer to the wall, to avoid any water or garbage that might be in the street. *What claim is Sampson making about himself and anyone from the rival house of Montague?*

17-28 Sampson's tough talk includes boasts about his ability to overpower women.

33 *poor-John:* a salted fish, considered fit only for poor people to eat.

35 During the next few speeches in this comic scene, watch what happens when the foolish, boastful servants actually meet their rivals face to face.

39 *marry:* a short form of "by the Virgin Mary" and so a mild swear word.

Sampson. A dog of that house shall move me to stand. I will take the wall of any man or maid of Montague's.

15   **Gregory.** That shows thee a weak slave, for the weakest goes to the wall.

Sampson. 'Tis true; and therefore women, being the weaker vessels, are ever thrust to the wall. Therefore I will push Montague's men from
20   the wall and thrust his maids to the wall.

Gregory. The quarrel is between our masters and us their men.

Sampson. 'Tis all one. I will show myself a tyrant. When I have fought with the men, I will be
25   cruel with the maids: I will cut off their heads.

Gregory. The heads of the maids?

Sampson. Ay, the heads of the maids, or their maidenheads. Take it in what sense thou wilt.

Gregory. They must take it in sense that feel it.

30   **Sampson.** Me they shall feel while I am able to stand; and 'tis known I am a pretty piece of flesh.

Gregory. 'Tis well thou art not fish; if thou hadst, thou hadst been poor-John. Draw thy tool! Here comes two of the house of Montagues.

[Enter Abram *and* Balthasar, *servants to the* Montagues.*]*

35   **Sampson.** My naked weapon is out. Quarrel! I will back thee.

Gregory. How? turn thy back and run?

Sampson. Fear me not.

Gregory. No, marry. I fear thee!

40   **Sampson.** Let us take the law of our sides; let them begin.

40-51 Gregory and Sampson decide to pick a fight by insulting the Montague servants with a rude gesture *(bite my thumb).* To appreciate the humor in this scene, think about what the servants say openly, what they say in asides, and what they actually do

49 *Aside:* privately, in a way that keeps the other characters from hearing what is said. Think of it as a whisper that the audience happens to overhear.

60-65 From the corner of his eye, Gregory can see Tybalt, a Capulet, arriving on the scene. With help on the way, his interest in fighting suddenly returns. He reminds Sampson to use *swashing,* or smashing, blows.

Gregory. I will frown as I pass by, and let them take it as they list.

Sampson. Nay, as they dare. I will bite my thumb at them; which is disgrace to them, if they bear it.

Abram. Do you bite your thumb at us, sir?

Sampson. I do bite my thumb, sir.

Abram. Do you bite your thumb at us, sir?

Sampson. *[Aside to* Gregory*]* Is the law of our side if I say ay?

Gregory. *[Aside to* Sampson*]* No.

Sampson. No, sir, I do not bite my thumb at you, sir; but I bite my thumb, sir.

Gregory. Do you quarrel, sir?

Abram. Quarrel, sir? No, sir.

Sampson. But if you do, sir, I am for you. I serve as good a man as you.

Abram. No better.

Sampson. Well, sir.

[Enter Benvolio, *nephew of* Montague *and first cousin of* Romeo.*]*

Gregory. *[Aside to* Sampson*]* Say "better." Here comes one of my master's kinsmen.

Sampson. Yes, better, sir.

Abram. You lie.

Sampson. Draw, if you be men. Gregory, remember thy swashing blow.

[They fight.]

66 As you read the next few lines, think about the different attitudes shown by Benvolio and Tybalt. *How would you describe the contrast between them?*

68-74 Tybalt misunderstands that Benvolio is trying to stop the fight. He challenges Benvolio.

68 *heartless hinds:* cowardly servants.

72 *drawn . . . peace:* You have your sword out, and yet you have the nerve to talk of peace?

74 *Have at thee:* Defend yourself.

75 *bills and partisans:* spears.

81-88 *A crutch . . . sword:* You need a crutch more than a sword. *How do both wives respond to their husbands' "fighting words"?*

Benvolio. Part, fools! *[Beats down their swords.]* Put
    up your swords. You know not what you do.

[Enter Tybalt, *hot-headed nephew of* Lady Capulet
and first cousin of Juliet.*]*

Tybalt. What, art thou drawn among these heartless
    hinds? Turn thee, Benvolio! look upon thy death.

70 **Benvolio.** I do but keep the peace. Put up thy sword,
    Or manage it to part these men with me.

Tybalt. What, drawn, and talk of peace? I hate the word
    As I hate hell, all Montagues, and thee.
    Have at thee, coward!

[They fight.]

*[Enter several of both houses, who join the fray; then
enter* Citizens *and* Peace Officers, *with clubs.]*

75 **Officer.** Clubs, bills, and partisans! Strike! beat them
    down!

Citizens. Down with the Capulets! Down with the
    Montagues!

[Enter old Capulet *and* Lady Capulet.*]*

Capulet. What noise is this? Give me my long sword,
80   ho!

Lady Capulet. A crutch, a crutch! Why call you for
    a sword?

Capulet. My sword, I say! Old Montague is come
    And flourishes his blade in spite of me.

[Enter old Montague *and* Lady Montague.*]*

85 **Montague.** Thou villain Capulet!—Hold me not, let
    me go.

Lady Montague. Thou shalt not stir one foot to
    seek a foe.

89-96 The Prince is furious about the street fighting caused by the feud. He commands all the men to put down their weapons and pay attention.
pernicious: destructive.

97-103 ***Three . . . hate:*** The Prince holds Capulet and Montague responsible for three recent street fights, probably started by an offhand remark or insult ***(airy word).*** He warns the old men that they will be put to death if any more fights occur.

Exeunt *(Latin):* they leave. When one person leaves the stage, the direction is *Exit.*

112 ***Who . . . abroach:*** Who reopened this old argument?

114 ***adversary:*** enemy.

115 ***ere:*** before.

[Enter Prince Escalus, with attendants. At first no one hears him.]

Prince. Rebellious subjects, enemies to peace,
90   Profaners of this neighbor-stained steel—
Will they not hear? What, ho! you men, you beasts,
That quench the fire of your pernicious rage
With purple fountains issuing from your veins!
On pain of torture, from those bloody hands
95   Throw your mistempered weapons to the ground
And hear the sentence of your moved prince.
Three civil brawls, bred of an airy word
By thee, old Capulet, and Montague,
Have thrice disturbed the quiet of our streets
100   And made Verona's ancient citizens
Cast by their grave beseeming ornaments
To wield old partisans, in hands as old,
Cankered with peace, to part your cankered hate.
If ever you disturb our streets again,
105   Your lives shall pay the forfeit of the peace.
For this time all the rest depart away.
You, Capulet, shall go along with me;
And, Montague, come you this afternoon,
To know our farther pleasure in this case,
110   To old Freetown, our common judgment place.
Once more, on pain of death, all men depart.

[Exeunt all but Montague, Lady Montague, and Benvolio.]

Montague. Who set this ancient quarrel new
abroach? Speak, nephew, were you by when it
began?

Benvolio. Here were the servants of your adversary
115   And yours, close fighting ere I did approach.
I drew to part them. In the instant came
The fiery Tybalt, with his sword prepared;
Which, as he breathed defiance to my ears,
He swung about his head and cut the winds,

120 *withal:* by this.

122 *on part and part:* some on one side, some on the other.

114-123 *According to Benvolio, what kind of person is Tybalt? How might Tybalt be likely to act if he meets Benvolio again?*

125 *fray:* fight.

128 *drave:* drove.

130 *rooteth:* grows.

132-138 *made:* moved; *covert:* covering. Romeo saw Benvolio coming toward him and hid in the woods. Benvolio decided to respect Romeo's privacy and went away. *What does this action tell you about Benvolio?*

139-150 Romeo has been wandering through the woods at night, often in tears. At daybreak he returns home and locks himself in his darkened room. Montague is deeply concerned about his son's behavior and feels he needs guidance.

153 *importuned:* demanded.

120 Who, nothing hurt withal, hissed him in scorn.
While we were interchanging thrusts and blows,
Came more and more, and fought on part and part,
Till the Prince came, who parted either part.

Lady Montague. O, where is Romeo? Saw you him
125 today? Right glad I am he was not at this fray.

Benvolio. Madam, an hour before the worshiped sun
Peered forth the golden window of the East,
A troubled mind drave me to walk abroad,
Where, underneath the grove of sycamore
130 That westward rooteth from the city's side,
So early walking did I see your son.
Towards him I made, but he was ware of me
And stole into the covert of the wood.
I—measuring his affections by my own,
135 Which then most sought where most might not be
found,
Being one too many by my weary self—
Pursued my humor, not pursuing his,
And gladly shunned who gladly fled from me.

Montague. Many a morning hath he there been seen,
140 With tears augmenting the fresh morning's dew,
Adding to clouds more clouds with his deep sighs; *
But all so soon as the all-cheering sun
Should in the farthest East begin to draw
The shady curtains from Aurora's bed,
145 Away from light steals home my heavy son
And private in his chamber pens himself,
Shuts up his windows, locks fair daylight out,
And makes himself an artificial night.
Black and portentous must this humor prove
150 Unless good counsel may the cause remove.

Benvolio. My noble uncle, do you know the cause?

Montague. I neither know it nor can learn of him.

Benvolio. Have you importuned him by any means?

155 *his own affections' counselor:* Romeo keeps to himself.

158-163 *So far from . . . know:* Finding out what Romeo is thinking is nearly impossible. Montague compares his son to a young bud destroyed by the bite of an envious worm. He wants to find out what is bothering Romeo so he can help him.

167 *shrift:* confession.

168 *cousin:* any relative or close friend. The informal version is *coz.*

175-180 *Why has Romeo been so depressed?*

Montague. Both by myself and many other friends;
155   But he, his own affections' counselor,
    Is to himself—I will not say how true—
    But to himself so secret and so close,
    So far from sounding and discovery,
    As is the bud bit with an envious worm
160   Ere he can spread his sweet leaves to the air
    Or dedicate his beauty to the sun.
    Could we but learn from whence his sorrows grow,
    We would as willingly give cure as know.

[Enter Romeo lost in thought.]

Benvolio. See, where he comes. So please you step
165   aside, I'll know his grievance, or be much denied.

Montague. I would thou wert so happy by thy stay
    To hear true shrift. Come, madam, let's away.

[Exeunt Montague and Lady.]

Benvolio. Good morrow, cousin.

Romeo.   Is the day so young?

170 **Benvolio.** But new struck nine.

Romeo.   Ay me! sad hours seem long.
    Was that my father that went hence so fast?

Benvolio. It was. What sadness lengthens Romeo's
    hours?

175 **Romeo.** Not having that which having makes them
    short.

Benvolio. In love?

Romeo. Out—

Benvolio. Of love?

180 **Romeo.** Out of her favor where I am in love.

181-184 *love:* refers to Cupid, the god of love. Cupid is pictured as a blind boy with wings and a bow and arrow. Anyone hit by one of his arrows falls in love instantly. Since he is blind, love is blind. He looks gentle, but in reality he can be a harsh master.

188-196 Romeo, confused and upset, tries to describe his feelings about love in phrases like "loving hate." Look for other expressions in this speech made up of pairs of words that contradict each other. *Has love ever made you feel this way?*

197-204 Benvolio expresses his sympathy for Romeo. Romeo replies that this is one more problem caused by love. He now feels worse than before because he must carry the weight of Benvolio's sympathy along with his own grief.

206 *purged:* cleansed (of the smoke).

207 *vexed:* troubled.

211 *Soft:* Wait a minute.

Benvolio. Alas that love, so gentle in his view,
Should be so tyrannous and rough in proof!

Romeo. Alas that love, whose view is muffled still,
Should without eyes see pathways to his will!
185 Where shall we dine?—O me! What fray was
here?—
Yet tell me not, for I have heard it all.
Here's much to do with hate, but more with love.
Why then, O brawling love! O loving hate!
190 O anything, of nothing first create!
O heavy lightness! serious vanity!
Misshapen chaos of well-seeming forms!
Feather of lead, bright smoke, cold fire, sick health!
Still-waking sleep, that is not what it is!
195 This love feel I, that feel no love in this.
Dost thou not laugh?

Benvolio. No, coz, I rather weep.

Romeo. Good heart, at what?

Benvolio. At thy good heart's oppression.

200 **Romeo.** Why, such is love's transgression.
Griefs of mine own lie heavy in my breast,
Which thou wilt propagate, to have it prest
With more of thine. This love that thou hast shown
Doth add more grief to too much of mine own.
205 Love is a smoke raised with the fume of sighs;
Being purged, a fire sparkling in lovers' eyes;
Being vexed, a sea nourished with lovers' tears.
What is it else? A madness most discreet,
A choking gall, and a preserving sweet.
210 Farewell, my coz.

Benvolio. Soft! I will go along.
An if you leave me so, you do me wrong.

Romeo. Tut! I have lost myself; I am not here:
This is not Romeo, he's some other where.

215 *sadness:* seriousness

221-222 Romeo seems unaware of how foolish his dramatic confession sounds. Benvolio responds with appropriate but gentle sarcasm.

222-225 Romeo and Benvolio talk of love in terms of archery, another reference to Cupid and his love arrows.

225-228 *She'll . . . unharmed:* The girl isn't interested in falling in love. She is like Diana, the goddess of chastity, the moon, and the hunt, who avoided Cupid's arrows.

229-231 She is unmoved by Romeo's declaration of love, his adoring looks, and his wealth.

234-238 Since she has vowed to remain chaste, she will die without children, and her beauty will not be passed on to future generations *(posterity).*

240-241 *To merit . . . despair:* The girl will reach heaven *(bliss)* by being chaste, which causes Romeo *despair,* or hopelessness. *forsworn to:* sworn not to.

245-246 *What is Benvolio's advice?*

Benvolio. Tell me in sadness, who is that you love?

Romeo. What, shall I groan and tell thee?

Benvolio.   Groan? Why, no;
  But sadly tell me who.

Romeo. Bid a sick man in sadness make his will.
  Ah, word ill urged to one that is so ill!
  In sadness, cousin, I do love a woman.

Benvolio. I aimed so near when I supposed you loved.

Romeo. A right good markman! And she's fair I love.

Benvolio. A right fair mark, fair coz, is soonest hit.

Romeo. Well, in that hit you miss. She'll not be hit
  With Cupid's arrow. She hath Dian's wit,
  And, in strong proof of chastity well armed,
  From Love's weak childish bow she lives unharmed.
  She will not stay the siege of loving terms,
  Nor bide the encounter of assailing eyes,
  Nor ope her lap to saint-seducing gold.
  O, she is rich in beauty; only poor
  That, when she dies, with beauty dies her store.

Benvolio. Then she hath sworn that she will still live
  chaste?

Romeo. She hath, and in that sparing makes huge waste;
  For beauty, starved with her severity,
  Cuts beauty off from all posterity.
  She is too fair, too wise, wisely too fair,
  To merit bliss by making me despair.
  She hath forsworn to love, and in that vow
  Do I live dead that live to tell it now.

Benvolio. Be ruled by me: forget to think of her.

Romeo. O, teach me how I should forget to think!

Benvolio. By giving liberty unto thine eyes:
  Examine other beauties.

247-248 *'Tis . . . more:* That would only make me appreciate my own love's beauty more.

249 Masks were worn by Elizabethan women to protect their complexions from the sun.

257 *I'll pay . . . debt:* I'll convince you you're wrong, or die trying.

1 *bound:* obligated.

4 *reckoning:* reputation.

6 *what say . . . suit:* Paris is asking for Capulet's response to his proposal to marry Juliet.

Romeo.   'Tis the way
To call hers (exquisite) in question more.
These happy masks that kiss fair ladies' brows,
250   Being black, puts us in mind they hide the fair.
He that is strucken blind cannot forget
The precious treasure of his eyesight lost.
Show me a mistress that is passing fair,
What doth her beauty serve but as a note
255   Where I may read who passed that passing fair?
Farewell. Thou canst not teach me to forget.

Benvolio. I'll pay that doctrine, or else die in debt.

[Exeunt.]

Scene 2 *A street near the Capulet house.*

> *This scene opens with Count Paris, a young nobleman, asking Capulet for permission to marry his daughter, Juliet. Capulet says that Juliet is too young but gives Paris permission to court her and try to win her favor. He also invites Paris to a party he is giving that night.*

> *Romeo finds out about the party and discovers that Rosaline, the girl who rejected him, will be present. Benvolio urges Romeo to go to the party to see how Rosaline compares with the other women.*

[Enter Capulet with Paris, a kinsman of the Prince, and Servant.]

Capulet. But Montague is bound as well as I,
In penalty alike; and 'tis not hard, I think,
For men so old as we to keep the peace.

Paris. Of honorable reckoning are you both,
5   And pity 'tis you lived at odds so long.
But now, my lord, what say you to my suit?

Capulet. But saying o'er what I have said before:

8-13 ***My child . . . made:*** Capulet repeats his claim that Juliet, still thirteen, is too young for marriage. He further argues that girls are hurt by becoming mothers too soon.

14 ***The earth . . . she:*** All my children are dead except Juliet.

16 ***woo her:*** try to win her affection.

18-19 ***An . . . voice:*** I will give my approval to the one she chooses.

20 ***old accustomed feast:*** a traditional or annual party.

29-33 ***Among . . . none:*** Tonight at the party you will witness ***(inherit)*** the loveliest young girls in Verona, including Juliet. When you see all of them together, your opinion of Juliet may change.

35 ***sirrah:*** a term used to address a servant.

38 ***My house . . . stay:*** My house and my welcome wait for their pleasure. *What does Capulet send the servant to do?*

39-42 The servant is bewildered and frustrated because he has been asked to read—a skill he does not have. He confuses the craftsmen and their tools, tapping a typical source of humor for Elizabethan clowns, then goes off to seek help.

My child is yet a stranger in the world,
She hath not seen the change of fourteen years;
10 Let two more summers wither in their pride
Ere we may think her ripe to be a bride.

Paris. Younger than she are happy mothers made.

Capulet. And too soon marred are those so early made.
The earth hath swallowed all my hopes but she;
15 She is the hopeful lady of my earth.
But woo her, gentle Paris, get her heart;
My will to her consent is but a part.
An she agree, within her scope of choice
Lies my consent and fair according voice.
20 This night I hold an old accustomed feast,
Whereto I have invited many a guest,
Such as I love, and you among the store,
One more, most welcome, makes my number more.
At my poor house look to behold this night
25 Earth-treading stars that make dark heaven light.
Such comfort as do lusty young men feel
When well-appareled April on the heel
Of limping Winter treads, even such delight
Among fresh female buds shall you this night
30 Inherit at my house. Hear all, all see,
And like her most whose merit most shall be;
Which, on more view of many, mine, being one,
May stand in number, though in reck'ning none.
Come, go with me. *[To* Servant, *giving him a paper.]*
35   Go, sirrah, trudge about
Through fair Verona; find those persons out
Whose names are written there, and to them say,
My house and welcome on their pleasure stay.

[Exeunt Capulet *and* Paris.]

Servant. Find them out whose names are written here!
40   It is written that the shoemaker should meddle with
his yard and the tailor with his last, the fisher with
his pencil and the painter with his nets; but I am

45-46 *In good time:* What luck; he is referring to the arrival of Romeo and Benvolio, who look like men who can read.

47-53 *Tut, man . . . die:* Benvolio is still trying to convince Romeo that the best way he can be helped *(holp)* in his love for Rosaline is to find someone else. Notice that he compares love to a disease that can only be cured by another disease.

58-61 Romeo is giving Benvolio a dismal picture of how he feels when he is interrupted by Capulet's servant. *God-den:* good evening.

62 *God gi' go-den:* God give you a good evening.

67 *Rest you merry:* Stay happy; a polite form of *goodbye.*

sent to find those persons whose names are here
writ, and can never find what names the writing
45   person hath here writ. I must to the learned. In
good time!

[Enter Benvolio and Romeo.]

Benvolio. Tut, man, one fire burns out another's
   ~ burning;
   One pain is lessened by another's anguish;
50   Turn giddy, and be holp by backward turning;
   One desperate grief cures with another's languish.
   Take thou some new infection to thy eye,
   And the rank poison of the old will die.

Romeo. Your plantain leaf is excellent for that.

55   **Benvolio.** For what, I pray thee?

Romeo.   For your broken shin.

Benvolio. Why, Romeo, art thou mad?

Romeo. Not mad, but bound more than a madman is;
   Shut up in prison, kept without my food,
60   Whipped and tormented and—God-den, good
      fellow.

Servant. God gi' go-den. I pray, sir, can you read?

Romeo. Ay, mine own fortune in my misery.

Servant. Perhaps you have learned it without book.
65   But I pray, can you read anything you see?

Romeo. Ay, if I know the letters and the language.

Servant. Ye say honestly. Rest you merry!

*[Romeo's joking goes over the clown's head. He
concludes that Romeo cannot read and prepares to seek
someone who can.]*

Romeo. Stay, fellow; I can read.   *[He reads.]*
   "Signior Martino and his wife and daughters;

75 Notice that Romeo's beloved Rosaline, a Capulet, is
invited to the party. (This is the first time in the play
that her name is mentioned.) Mercutio, a friend of
both Romeo and the Capulets, is also invited.

78 *Whither:* where.

87-88 *crush a cup of wine:* slang for "drink some wine."

92-94 *Go . . . crow:* Go to the party and, with unbiased
eyes, compare Rosaline with the other beautiful girls.

95-98 *When . . . liars:* If the love I have for Rosaline, which
is like a religion, changes because of such lies (that
others could be more beautiful), let my tears be turned
to fire and my eyes be burned. *To what does Romeo
compare Rosaline's beauty?*

70 County Anselmo and his beauteous sisters;
The lady widow of Vitruvio;
Signior Placentio and his lovely nieces;
Mercutio and his brother Valentine;
Mine uncle Capulet, his wife, and daughters;
75 My fair niece Rosaline and Livia;
Signior Valentio and his cousin Tybalt;
Lucio and the lively Helena."

[Gives back the paper.]
A fair assembly. Whither should they come?

Servant. Up.

80 **Romeo.** Whither?

Servant. To supper, to our house.

Romeo. Whose house?

Servant. My master's.

Romeo. Indeed I should have asked you that before.

85 **Servant.** Now I'll tell you without asking. My master
is the great rich Capulet; and if you be not of the
house of Montagues, I pray come and crush a cup
of wine. Rest you merry!

[Exit.]

Benvolio. At this same ancient feast of Capulet's
90 Sups the fair Rosaline whom thou so lovest,
With all the admired beauties of Verona.
Go thither, and with unattainted eye
Compare her face with some that I shall show,
And I will make thee think thy swan a crow.

95 **Romeo.** When the devout religion of mine eye
Maintains such falsehood, then turn tears to fires;
And these, who, often drowned, could never die,
Transparent heretics, be burnt for liars!
One fairer than my love? The all-seeing sun

101-106 *Tut . . . best:* You've seen Rosaline alone; now compare her with some other woman. *How does Benvolio think Rosaline will stack up against the other girls?*

107-108 Romeo agrees to go to the party, but only to see Rosaline.

4-5 *What:* a call like "Hey, where are you?"

100   Ne'er saw her match since first the world begun.

Benvolio. Tut! you saw her fair, none else being by,
        Herself poised with herself in either eye;
        But in that crystal scales let there be weighed
        Your lady's love against some other maid
105   That I will show you shining at this feast,
        And she shall scant show well that now shows best.

Romeo. I'll go along, no such sight to be shown,
        But to rejoice in splendor of mine own.

[Exeunt.]

Scene 3 *Capulet's house.*

*In this scene, you will meet Juliet, her mother,
and her nurse. The Nurse, a merry and slightly
crude servant, has been in charge of Juliet
since her birth. Once she starts talking, she
can't stop. Just before the party, Juliet's
mother asks if Juliet has thought about getting
married. Lady Capulet is matchmaking, trying
to convince her daughter that Paris would
make a good husband. Juliet responds just as
you might if your parents set up a blind date
for you—without much enthusiasm.*

[Enter Lady Capulet *and* Nurse.*]*

Lady Capulet. Nurse, where's my daughter? Call her
        forth to me.

Nurse. Now, by my maidenhead at twelve year old,
        I bade her come. What, lamb! what, ladybird!
5   God forbid! Where's this girl? What, Juliet!

[Enter Juliet.*]*

Juliet. How now? Who calls?

Nurse. Your mother.

9-12 ***give leave . . . counsel:*** Lady Capulet seems flustered or nervous. First she tells the Nurse to leave, then she remembers that the Nurse knows Juliet as well as anyone and asks her to stay and listen. ***of a pretty age:*** of an attractive age, ready for marriage.

17 ***teen:*** sorrow.

19 ***Lammastide:*** August 1, a religious feast day and the day after Juliet's birthday. The feast day is now a little more than two weeks ***(a fortnight)*** away.

21-54 The Nurse now begins to babble on about various memories of Juliet's childhood. She talks of her dead daughter, Susan, who was the same age as Juliet. Susan probably died in infancy, allowing for the Nurse to become a wet nurse to (breast-feed) Juliet. She remembers an earthquake that happened on the day she stopped breast-feeding Juliet ***(she was weaned).***

31 ***laid wormwood to my dug:*** applied wormwood, a plant with a bitter taste, to her breast in order to discourage the child from breast-feeding.

37 ***tetchy:*** touchy; cranky.

38-39 ***Shake . . . trudge:*** When the dovehouse shook, I knew enough to leave.

41 ***by the rood:*** The rood is the cross on which Christ was crucified. The expression means something like "by God."

Juliet. Madam, I am here. What is your will?

Lady Capulet. This is the matter—Nurse, give leave
10   awhile,
We must talk in secret. Nurse, come back again;
I have remembered me, thou's hear our counsel.
Thou knowest my daughter's of a pretty age.

Nurse. Faith, I can tell her age unto an hour.

15 **Lady Capulet.** She's not fourteen.

Nurse.   I'll lay fourteen of my teeth—
And yet, to my teen be it spoken, I have but four—
She's not fourteen. How long is it now
To Lammastide?

20 **Lady Capulet.** A fortnight and odd days.

Nurse. Even or odd, of all days in the year,
Come Lammas Eve at night shall she be fourteen.
Susan and she (God rest all Christian souls!)
Were of an age. Well, Susan is with God;
25   She was too good for me. But, as I said,
On Lammas Eve at night shall she be fourteen;
That shall she, marry; I remember it well.
'Tis since the earthquake now eleven years;
And she was weaned (I never shall forget it),
30   Of all the days of the year, upon that day.
For I had then laid wormwood to my dug,
Sitting in the sun under the dovehouse wall.
My lord and you were then at Mantua—
Nay, I do bear a brain—But, as I said,
35   When it did taste the wormwood on the nipple
Of my dug and felt it bitter, pretty fool,
To see it tetchy and fall out with the dug!
Shake, quoth the dovehouse! 'Twas no need, I trow,
To bid me trudge.
40   And since that time it is eleven years,
For then she could stand alone; nay, by the rood,

43 *broke her brow:* cut her forehead.

46-54 *"Yea" . . . "Ay":* To quiet Juliet after her fall, the Nurse's husband makes a crude joke, asking the baby whether she'll fall the other way (on her back) when she's older. Although at three Juliet doesn't understand the question, she stops crying *(stinted)* and innocently answers, "Yes." The Nurse finds this story so funny, she can't stop retelling it.

67 *e'er:* ever.

70 Lady Capulet uses the word *marry* in two different senses. The first *marry* means "by the Virgin Mary"; the second means "to wed."

She could have run and waddled all about;
For even the day before, she broke her brow;
And then my husband (God be with his soul!
45   'A was a merry man) took up the child.
"Yea," quoth he, "dost thou fall upon thy face?
Thou wilt fall backward when thou has more wit,
Wilt thou not, Jule?" And, by my holidam,
The pretty wretch left crying, and said "Ay."
50   To see now how a jest shall come about!
I warrant, an I should live a thousand years,
I never should forget it. "Wilt thou not, Jule?"
   quoth he,
And, pretty fool, it stinted, and said "Ay."

55   **Lady Capulet.** Enough of this. I pray thee hold thy
   peace.

Nurse. Yes, madam. Yet I cannot choose but laugh
To think it should leave crying and say "Ay."
And yet, I warrant, it had upon its brow
60   A bump as big as a young cock'rel's stone;
A perilous knock; and it cried bitterly.
"Yea," quoth my husband, "fallst upon thy face?
Thou wilt fall backward when thou comest to age,
Wilt thou not, Jule?" It stinted, and said "Ay."

65   **Juliet.** And stint thou too, I pray thee, nurse, say I.

Nurse. Peace, I have done. God mark thee to his grace!
Thou wast the prettiest babe that e'er I nursed.
An I might live to see thee married once,
I have my wish.

70   **Lady Capulet.** Marry, that "marry" is the very theme
I came to talk of. Tell me, daughter Juliet,
How stands your disposition to be married?

Juliet. It is an honor that I dream not of.

Nurse. An honor? Were not I thine only nurse,
75   I would say thou hadst sucked wisdom from thy teat.

80-81 *I was . . . maid:* I was your mother at about your age, yet you are still unmarried.

84 *a man of wax:* a man so perfect he could be a wax statue. Sculptors used to use wax figures as models for their works.

91-98 *Read . . . cover:* Lady Capulet uses an extended metaphor that compares Paris to a book that Juliet should read. Look for the similarities she points out.

93 *several lineament:* separate feature. Lady Capulet points out how each of Paris' features makes the others look even better.

96 *margent . . . eyes:* She compares Paris' eyes to the margin of the page of a book where notes are written that explain the content.

97-100 *This . . . hide:* This beautiful book (Paris) only needs a cover (wife) to become even better. He may be hiding even more wonderful qualities inside.

105 The Nurse can't resist one of her earthy comments. She notes that women get bigger (pregnant) when they marry.

107 *I'll look . . . move:* Juliet's playful answer means "I'll look at him with the intention of liking him, if simply looking can make me like him."

Lady Capulet. Well, think of marriage now. Younger than you,
Here in Verona, ladies of esteem,
Are made already mothers. By my count,
80 I was your mother much upon these years
That you are now a maid. Thus then in brief:
The valiant Paris seeks you for his love.

Nurse. A man, young lady! lady, such a man
As all the world—why he's a man of wax.

85 **Lady Capulet.** Verona's summer hath not such a flower.

Nurse. Nay, he's a flower, in faith—a very flower.

Lady Capulet. What say you? Can you love the gentleman?
90 This night you shall behold him at our feast.
Read o'er the volume of young Paris' face,
And find delight writ there with beauty's pen;
Examine every several lineament,
And see how one another lends content;
95 And what obscured in this fair volume lies
Find written in the margent of his eyes.
This precious book of love, this unbound lover,
To beautify him only lacks a cover.
The fish lives in the sea, and 'tis much pride
100 For fair without the fair within to hide.
That book in many's eyes doth share the glory,
That in gold clasps locks in the golden story;
So shall you share all that he doth possess,
By having him making yourself no less.

105 **Nurse.** No less? Nay, bigger! Women grow by men.

Lady Capulet. Speak briefly, can you like of Paris' love?

Juliet. I'll look to like, if looking liking move;
But no more deep will I endart mine eye
Than your consent gives strength to make it fly.

113 *extremity:* confusion. The servant is upset because everything is happening at once, and he can't handle it. *straight:* immediately.

116 *the County stays:* Count Paris is waiting for you.

1-10 *shall this . . . be gone:* Romeo asks whether they should send a messenger announcing their arrival at the party. Benvolio replies that this custom is out of date. He then lists all the things they won't use to make such an announcement. For example, *We'll have . . . crowkeeper:* We won't send someone dressed as a blindfolded Cupid, carrying a bow and looking like a scarecrow. Let them think what they want. We'll *measure them a measure* (dance one dance with them) and go.

[Enter a Servingman.]

Servingman. Madam, the guests are come, supper
served up, you called, my young lady asked for, the
nurse cursed in the pantry, and everything in
extremity. I must hence to wait. I beseech you
follow straight.

Lady Capulet. We follow thee. *[Exit Servingman.]*
Juliet, the County stays.

Nurse. Go, girl, seek happy nights to happy days.

[Exeunt.]

Scene 4 *A street near the Capulet house.*

> It is the evening of the Capulet masque, or
> costume ball. Imagine the guests proceeding
> through the darkened streets with torches to
> light the way.
>
> Romeo and his two friends, Mercutio and
> Benvolio, join the procession. Their masks will
> prevent them from being recognized as
> Montagues. Mercutio and Benvolio are in a
> playful, partying mood, but Romeo is still
> depressed by his unanswered love for Rosaline.
> Romeo has also had a dream that warned him
> of the harmful consequences of this party. He
> senses trouble.
>
> *[Enter* Romeo, Mercutio, Benvolio, *with five or
> six other* Maskers; Torchbearers.*]*

Romeo. What, shall this speech be spoke for our
excuse? Or shall we on without apology?

Benvolio. The date is out of such prolixity.
We'll have no Cupid hoodwinked with a scarf,
Bearing a Tartar's painted bow of lath,
Scaring the ladies like a crowkeeper;
Nor no without-book prologue, faintly spoke

The Tragedy of Romeo and Juliet   43

12 *heavy:* sad. In spite of his mood, Romeo makes a joke based on the meanings of *heavy* and *light.*

13-33 As you read these lines, try to visualize each man. Romeo is overcome with sadness because of his lovestruck condition. Mercutio is determined to cheer him up. He is making fun of Romeo, but he is doing it in a friendly way.

30-33 *Give . . . for me:* Give me a mask for an ugly face. I don't care if people notice my ugliness. Here, look at my heavy eyebrows.

35 *betake . . . legs:* dance.

36-39 *Let . . . look on:* Let playful people tickle the grass *(rushes)* on the floor with their dancing. I'll stick with the old saying *(grandsire phrase)* and hold a candle and watch the dancers.

After the prompter, for our entrance;
But let them measure us by what they will,
10   We'll measure them a measure, and be gone.

Romeo. Give me a torch. I am not for this ambling;
Being but heavy, I will bear the light.

Mercutio. Nay, gentle Romeo, we must have you
dance.

15   **Romeo.** Not I, believe me. You have dancing shoes
With nimble soles; I have a soul of lead
So stakes me to the ground I cannot move.

Mercutio. You are a lover. Borrow Cupid's wings
And soar with them above a common bound.

20   **Romeo.** I am too sore enpierced with his shaft
To soar with his light feathers, and so bound
I cannot bound a pitch above dull woe.
Under love's heavy burden do I sink.

Mercutio. And, to sink in it, should you burden love—
25   Too great oppression for a tender thing.

Romeo. Is love a tender thing? It is too rough,
Too rude, too boist'rous, and it pricks like thorn.

Mercutio. If love be rough with you, be rough with love.
Prick love for pricking, and you beat love down.
30   Give me a case to put my visage in.
A visor for a visor! What care I
What curious eye doth quote deformities?
Here are the beetle brows shall blush for me.

Benvolio. Come, knock and enter, and no sooner in
35   But every man betake him to his legs.

Romeo. A torch for me! Let wantons light of heart
Tickle the senseless rushes with their heels;
For I am proverbed with a grandsire phrase,
I'll be a candle-holder and look on;
40   The game was ne'er so fair, and I am done.

41-45 *Tut . . . daylight:* Mercutio jokes using various meanings of the word **dun,** which sounds like Romeo's last word, **done.** He concludes by saying they should not waste time **(burn daylight).**

60-102 In this famous speech Mercutio tries to cheer up Romeo by spinning a tale about how Queen Mab brings dreams to people. Queen Mab, queen of the fairies, was a folktale character well known to Shakespeare's audience. Mercutio is a born storyteller. He dominates the stage with his vivid descriptions, puns, and satires of people and professions. Don't worry about understanding everything in the speech. Read it instead for the language Mercutio uses and the dreamlike scene he creates.

62 *agate stone:* jewel for a ring.

64 *atomies:* tiny creatures. Note the description of Mab's tiny and delicate carriage.

66 *spinners' legs:* spiders' legs.

68 *traces:* harness.

Mercutio. Tut, dun's the mouse, the constable's own
    word!
    If thou art Dun, we'll draw thee from the mire
    Of, save your reverence, love, wherein thou stickst
45   Up to the ears. Come, we burn daylight, ho!

Romeo. Nay, that's not so.

Mercutio.   I mean, sir, in delay
    We waste our lights in vain, like lamps by day.
    Take our good meaning, for our judgment sits
50   Five times in that ere once in our five wits.

Romeo. And we mean well in going to this masque;
    But 'tis no wit to go.

Mercutio. Why, may one ask?

Romeo. I dreamt a dream tonight.

55 **Mercutio.** And so did I.

Romeo. Well, what was yours?

Mercutio. That dreamers often lie.

Romeo. In bed asleep, while they do dream things
    true.

60 **Mercutio.** O, then I see Queen Mab hath been with you.
    She is the fairies' midwife, and she comes
    In shape no bigger than an agate stone
    On the forefinger of an alderman,
    Drawn with a team of little atomies
65   Athwart men's noses as they lie asleep;
    Her wagon spokes made of long spinners' legs,
    The cover, of the wings of grasshoppers;
    Her traces, of the smallest spider's web;
    Her collars, of the moonshine's wat'ry beams;
70   Her whip, of cricket's bone; the lash, of film;
    Her wagoner, a small grey-coated gnat,
    Not half so big as a round little worm
    Pricked from the lazy finger of a maid;

75 *joiner:* carpenter.

79-81 *What does Mab make lawyers and ladies dream of?*

84-85 *Sometime she . . . suit:* Sometimes Mab makes a member of the king's court dream of receiving the king's special favors.

88 *benefice:* well-paying position for a church parson.

91 *ambuscadoes:* ambushes; *Spanish blades:* high-quality Spanish swords.

96 *plaits:* braids.

105-112 *True . . . South:* Mercutio is trying to keep Romeo from taking his dreams too seriously.

Her chariot is an empty hazelnut,
75   Made by the joiner squirrel or old grub,
Time out o' mind the fairies' coachmakers.
And in this state she gallops night by night
Through lovers' brains, and then they dream of love;
O'er courtiers' knees, that dream on curtsies straight;
80   O'er lawyers' fingers, who straight dream on fees;
O'er ladies' lips, who straight on kisses dream,
Which oft the angry Mab with blisters plagues,
Because their breaths with sweetmeats tainted are.
Sometime she gallops o'er a courtier's nose,
85   And then dreams he of smelling out a suit,
And sometime comes she with a tithe-pig's tail
Tickling a parson's nose as 'a lies asleep,
Then dreams he of another benefice.
Sometime she driveth o'er a soldier's neck,
90   And then dreams he of cutting foreign throats,
Of breaches, ambuscadoes, Spanish blades,
Of healths five fathom deep; and then anon
Drums in his ear, at which he starts and wakes,
And being thus frighted, swears a prayer or two
95   And sleeps again. This is that very Mab
That plaits the manes of horses in the night
And bakes the elflocks in foul sluttish hairs,
Which once untangled much misfortune bodes.
This is the hag, when maids lie on their backs,
100   That presses them and learns them first to bear,
Making them women of good carriage.
This is she—

Romeo.   Peace, peace, Mercutio, peace!
Thou talkst of nothing.

105   **Mercutio.**   True, I talk of dreams;
Which are the children of an idle brain,
Begot of nothing but vain fantasy;
Which is as thin of substance as the air,
And more inconstant than the wind, who woos
110   Even now the frozen bosom of the North

116-121 *my mind . . . death:* Romeo will not be cheered. He fears that some terrible event, caused by the stars, will begin at the party. Remember the phrase "star-crossed lovers" from the prologue of this act.

1-16 The opening lines of the scene are a comic conversation among three servants as they do their work.

2 *trencher:* wooden plate.

And, being angered, puffs away from thence,
Turning his face to the dew-dropping South.

Benvolio. This wind you talk of blows us from
ourselves.
115 Supper is done, and we shall come too late.

Romeo. I fear, too early; for my mind misgives
Some consequence, yet hanging in the stars,
Shall bitterly begin his fearful date
With this night's revels and expire the term
120 Of a despised life, closed in my breast,
By some vile forfeit of untimely death.
But he that hath the steerage of my course
Direct my sail! On, lusty gentlemen!

Benvolio. Strike, drum.

[Exeunt.]

Scene 5 *A hall in Capulet's house; the scene of the party.*

*This is the scene of the party at which Romeo
and Juliet finally meet. Romeo and his friends,
disguised in their masks, arrive as uninvited
guests. As he watches the dancers, Romeo
suddenly sees Juliet and falls in love at first
sight. At the same time, Tybalt recognizes
Romeo's voice and knows he is a Montague.
He alerts Capulet and threatens to kill Romeo.
Capulet, however, insists that Tybalt behave
himself and act like a gentleman. Promising
revenge, Tybalt leaves. Romeo and Juliet meet
and kiss in the middle of the dance floor. Only
after they part do they learn each other's
identity.*

[Servingmen come forth with napkins.]

First Servingman. Where's Potpan, that he helps not to
take away? He shift a trencher! he scrape a trencher!

7-8 *plate:* silverware and plates. ***marchpane:*** marzipan, a sweet made from almond paste.

17-31 Capulet is welcoming his guests and inviting them all to dance. At the same time, like a good host, he is trying to get the party going. He alternates talking with his guests and telling the servants what to do.

21-22 *She that . . . corns:* Any woman too shy to dance will be assumed to have *corns,* ugly and painful growths on the toes.

24 *visor:* mask.

31-45 The dancing has begun, and Capulet and his relative are watching as they talk about days gone. *Although the two old men are speaking, whom do you think the audience is watching?*

Second Servingman. When good manners shall lie all
  in one or two men's hands, and they unwashed
5 too, 'tis a foul thing.

First Servingman. Away with the joint-stools, remove
  the court-cupboard, look to the plate. Good thou,
  save me a piece of marchpane and, as thou lovest
  me, let the porter let in Susan Grindstone and Nell.
10 Anthony, and Potpan!

Second Servingman. Ay, boy, ready.

First Servingman. You are looked for and called for,
  asked for and sought for, in the great chamber.

Third Servingman. We cannot be here and there too.
15 Cheerly, boys! Be brisk awhile, and the longer liver
  take all.

[Exeunt.]

[Maskers appear with Capulet, Lady Capulet, Juliet, *all the*
Guests, *and* Servants.*]*

Capulet. Welcome, gentlemen! Ladies that have their
    toes
    Unplagued with corns will have a bout with you.
20 Ah ha, my mistresses! which of you all
    Will now deny to dance? She that makes dainty,
    She I'll swear hath corns. Am I come near ye now?
    Welcome, gentlemen! I have seen the day
    That I have worn a visor and could tell
25 A whispering tale in a fair lady's ear,
    Such as would please. 'Tis gone, 'tis gone, 'tis gone!
    You are welcome, gentlemen! Come, musicians, play.
    A hall, a hall! give room! and foot it, girls.

[Music plays and they dance.]

    More light, you knaves! and turn the tables up,
30 And quench the fire, the room is grown too hot.
    Ah, sirrah, this unlooked-for sport comes well.
    Nay, sit, nay, sit, good cousin Capulet,

46-47 Romeo has spotted Juliet across the dance hall, and he is immediately hypnotized by her beauty.

51-52 *Ethiop's ear:* the ear of an Ethiopian (African). *for earth too dear:* too precious for this world.

55-58 *The measure . . . night:* When the dance is over, Romeo will "bless" his hand by touching that of this beautiful woman. He swears that he has never loved before this moment because he's never seen true beauty before. *What seems to be Romeo's standard for falling In love?*

59-64 Tybalt recognizes Romeo's voice and tells his servant to get his sword *(rapier)*. He thinks Romeo has come to mock *(fleer)* their party. *What does Tybalt want to do to Romeo?*

For you and I are past our dancing days.
How long is't now since last yourself and I
35   Were in a mask?

Second Capulet. By'r Lady, thirty years.

Capulet. What, man? 'Tis not so much, 'tis not so
    much!
    'Tis since the nuptial of Lucentio,
40   Come Pentecost as quickly as it will,
    Some five-and-twenty years, and then we masked.

Second Capulet. 'Tis more, 'tis more! His son is elder, sir;
    His son is thirty.

Capulet.   Will you tell me that?
45   His son was but a ward two years ago.

Romeo. *[To a* Servingman*]* What lady's that, which doth
    enrich the hand of yonder knight?

Servant. I know not, sir.

Romeo. O, she doth teach the torches to burn bright!
50   It seems she hangs upon the cheek of night
    Like a rich jewel in an Ethiop's ear—
    Beauty too rich for use, for earth too dear!
    So shows a snowy dove trooping with crows
    As yonder lady o'er her fellows shows.
55   The measure done, I'll watch her place of stand
    And, touching hers, make blessed my rude hand.
    Did my heart love till now? Forswear it, sight!
    For I ne'er saw true beauty till this night.

Tybalt. This, by his voice, should be a Montague.
60   Fetch me my rapier, boy. What, dares the slave
    Come hither, covered with an antic face,
    To fleer and scorn at our solemnity?
    Now, by the stock and honor of my kin,
    To strike him dead I hold it not a sin.

65 **Capulet.** Why, how now, kinsman? Wherefore storm
    you so?

72-101 Capulet is not concerned about Romeo's presence and
notes that the boy has a reputation for being well-
mannered. He insists that Tybalt calm down and enjoy
the party.

85 ***goodman boy:*** a term used to address an inferior. In
an angrier tone Capulet tells Tybalt that he's acting
childishly and in an ungentlemanly manner.
Go to: Stop, that's enough!

89 ***set cock-a-hoop:*** cause everything to be upset.

93-94 ***scathe:*** harm; ***what:*** what I'm doing. You dare to
challenge my authority?

95-97 Capulet interrupts his angry speech with concerned
comments to his guests and servants.

98-101 ***Patience . . . gall:*** Tybalt says he will restrain himself,
being forced to; but his suppressed anger ***(choler)***
makes his body shake. *What do you think he might do
about his anger?*

Tybalt. Uncle, this is a Montague, our foe;
A villain, that is hither come in spite
To scorn at our solemnity this night.

70 **Capulet.** Young Romeo is it?

Tybalt.   'Tis he, that villain Romeo.

Capulet. Content thee, gentle coz, let him alone.
'A bears him like a portly gentleman,
And, to say truth, Verona brags of him
75 To be a virtuous and well-governed youth.
I would not for the wealth of all this town
Here in my house do him disparagement.
Therefore be patient, take no note of him.
It is my will; the which if thou respect,
80 Show a fair presence and put off these frowns,
An ill-beseeming semblance for a feast.

Tybalt. It fits when such a villain is a guest.
I'll not endure him.

Capulet.   He shall be endured.
85 What, goodman boy? I say he shall. Go to!
Am I the master here, or you? Go to!
You'll not endure him? God shall mend my soul!
You'll make a mutiny among my guests!
You will set cock-a-hoop! You'll be the man.

90 **Tybalt.** Why, uncle, 'tis a shame.

Capulet.   Go to, go to!
You are a saucy boy. Is't so, indeed?
This trick may chance to scathe you. I know what.
You must contrary me! Marry, 'tis time.—
95 Well said, my hearts!—You are a princox—go!
Be quiet, or—More light, more light!—For shame!
I'll make you quiet; what!—Cheerly, my hearts!

Tybalt. Patience perforce with willful choler meeting
Makes my flesh tremble in their different greeting.
100 I will withdraw; but this intrusion shall,

102-121 Think of this part of the scene as a close-up involving only Romeo and Juliet. With the party going on around them, Romeo and Juliet are at center stage, ignoring everyone else. They touch the palms of their hands together. Their conversation revolves around Romeo's comparison of his lips to pilgrims *(palmers)* who have traveled to visit a holy shrine, Juliet. Juliet goes along with his comparison because she feels the same way he does.

118 In the midst of the dancers, Romeo kisses Juliet.

122 *kiss by the book:* Juliet could mean "You kiss like an expert, someone who has studied the correct method." Or she could be teasing Romeo, meaning "You kiss coldly, as though you had learned it by reading a book."

123-130 Because of the Nurse's message from Lady Capulet, Juliet leaves, and Romeo is left to talk with the Nurse. She informs him that Juliet is Capulet's daughter and a good catch—whoever wins her shall become rich *(have the chinks).*

Now seeming sweet, convert to bitter gall.

[Exit.]

Romeo. If I profane with my unworthiest hand
This holy shrine, the gentle fine is this:
My lips, two blushing pilgrims, ready stand
105   To smooth that rough touch with a tender kiss.

Juliet. Good pilgrim, you do wrong your hand too
    much,
Which mannerly devotion shows in this;
For saints have hands that pilgrims' hands do touch,
110   And palm to palm is holy palmers' kiss.

Romeo. Have not saints lips, and holy palmers too?

Juliet. Ay, pilgrim, lips that they must use in prayer.

Romeo. O, then, dear saint, let lips do what hands do!
They pray; grant thou, lest faith turn to despair.

115   **Juliet.** Saints do not move, though grant for prayers'
    sake.

Romeo. Then move not while my prayer's effect I take.
Thus from my lips, by thine my sin is purged.

[Kisses her.]

Juliet. Then have my lips the sin that they have took.

120   **Romeo.** Sin from my lips? O trespass sweetly urged!
Give me my sin again.

[Kisses her.]

Juliet. You kiss by the book.

Nurse. Madam, your mother craves a word with you.

Romeo. What is her mother?

125   **Nurse.**   Marry, bachelor,
Her mother is the lady of the house.

132 *my life . . . debt:* my life belongs to my enemy. *How does Romeo react when he learns that Juliet is Capulet's daughter?*

136 *towards:* coming up.

143-148 Juliet asks the Nurse to identify various guests as they leave the house. *What does she really want to know?*

151 In this line Juliet tells her own fortune, although she doesn't know it.

And a good lady, and a wise and virtuous.
I nursed her daughter that you talked withal.
I tell you, he that can lay hold of her
130   Shall have the chinks.

Romeo.   Is she a Capulet?
O dear account! my life is my foe's debt.

Benvolio. Away, be gone, the sport is at the best.

Romeo. Ay, so I fear; the more is my unrest.

135 **Capulet.** Nay, gentlemen, prepare not to be gone;
We have a trifling foolish banquet towards.

[They whisper in his ear.]

Is it e'en so? Why then, I thank you all.
I thank you, honest gentlemen. Good night.
More torches here! *[Exeunt* Maskers.*]* Come on then,
140   let's to bed.
Ah, sirrah, by my fay, it waxes late;
I'll to my rest.

[Exeunt all but Juliet *and* Nurse.*]*

Juliet. Come hither, nurse. What is yond gentleman?

Nurse. The son and heir of old Tiberio.

145 **Juliet.** What's he that now is going out of door?

Nurse. Marry, that, I think, be young Petruchio.

Juliet. What's he that follows there, that would not
      dance?

Nurse. I know not.

150 **Juliet.** Go ask his name.—If he be married,
My grave is like to be my wedding bed.

Nurse. His name is Romeo, and a Montague,
The only son of your great enemy.

Juliet. My only love, sprung from my only hate!

155-156 ***Too early . . . too late:*** I fell in love with him before I learned who he is. ***Prodigious:*** abnormal, unlucky.

157 *How does Juliet feel about the fact that she's fallen in love with the son of her father's enemy?*

1-4 ***old . . . heir:*** Romeo's love for Rosaline *(old desire)* is now dead. His new love *(young affection)* replaces the old. Compared to Juliet, Rosaline no longer seems so lovely.

6 *What attracted Romeo and Juliet to each other?*

7 ***But . . . complain:*** Juliet, a Capulet, is Romeo's enemy; yet she is the one to whom he must plead *(complain)* his love.

9-12 *What problem now faces Romeo and Juliet?*

14 ***Temp'ring . . . sweet:*** moderating great difficulties with extreme delights.

155 Too early seen unknown, and known too late!
Prodigious birth of love it is to me
That I must love a loathed enemy.

Nurse. What's this? what's this?

Juliet.   A rhyme I learnt even now
160 Of one I danced withal.

[One calls within, "Juliet."]

Nurse. Anon, anon!
Come, let's away; the strangers all are gone.

[Exeunt.]

PROLOGUE

In a sonnet the CHORUS *summarizes what has happened so far in the play. He reviews how Romeo and Juliet have fallen in love and suggests both the problems and delights they now face. He also includes hints about what will result from the events of Act One.*

[Enter Chorus.]

Chorus. Now old desire doth in his deathbed lie,
And young affection gapes to be his heir.
That fair for which love groaned for and would die,
With tender Juliet matched, is now not fair.
5 Now Romeo is beloved, and loves again,
Alike bewitched by the charm of looks;
But to his foe supposed he must complain,
And she steal love's sweet bait from fearful hooks.
Being held a foe, he may not have access
10 To breathe such vows as lovers use to swear,
And she as much in love, her means much less
To meet her new beloved anywhere;
But passion lends them power, time means, to meet,
Temp'ring extremities with extreme sweet.
[Exit.]

1-2 ***Can . . . out:*** How can I leave when Juliet is still here? My body ***(dull earth)*** has to find its heart ***(center).***

8 ***conjure:*** use magic to call him.

10-23 ***Appear . . . us:*** Mercutio makes a series of loud jokes about Romeo's lovesickness. He tries to make Romeo appear by teasing him and suggestively naming parts of Rosaline's body. ***demesnes:*** areas.

ACT TWO

Scene 1 *A lane by the wall of Capulet's orchard.*

Later in the evening of the party, Romeo returns alone to the Capulet home, hoping for another glimpse of Juliet. He climbs the wall and hides outside, in the orchard. Meanwhile, Benvolio and Mercutio come looking for him, but he remains hidden behind the wall. Mercutio makes fun of Romeo and his lovesick condition. Keep in mind that Mercutio and Benvolio think Romeo is still in love with Rosaline, since they know nothing about his meeting with Juliet.

[Enter Romeo alone.]

Romeo. Can I go forward when my heart is here?
Turn back, dull earth, and find thy center out.

[Climbs the wall and leaps down within it.]

[Enter Benvolio with Mercutio.]

Benvolio. Romeo! my cousin Romeo! Romeo!

Mercutio. He is wise,
5 And, on my life, hath stol'n him home to bed.

Benvolio. He ran this way, and leapt this orchard wall.
Call, good Mercutio.

Mercutio.   Nay, I'll conjure too.
Romeo! humors! madman! passion! lover!
10 Appear thou in the likeness of a sigh;
Speak but one rhyme, and I am satisfied!
Cry but "Ay me!" pronounce but "love" and "dove";
Speak to my gossip Venus one fair word,

25-31 **'Twould . . . raise up him:** It would anger him if I called a stranger to join his lover **(mistress),** but I'm only calling Romeo to join her.

33 **To be . . . night:** to join with the night, which is as gloomy as Romeo is.

36 **medlar:** a fruit that looks like a small, brown apple.

41-45 **Romeo . . . found:** Mercutio jokes that he will go to his child's bed **(truckle bed)** since he is so "innocent."

One nickname for her purblind son and heir,
15   Young Adam Cupid, he that shot so trim
When King Cophetua loved the beggar maid!
He heareth not, he stirreth not, he moveth not;
The ape is dead, and I must conjure him.
I conjure thee by Rosaline's bright eyes,
20   By her high forehead and her scarlet lip,
By her fine foot, straight leg, and quivering thigh,
And the demesnes that there adjacent lie,
That in thy likeness thou appear to us!

Benvolio. An if he hear thee, thou wilt anger him.

25 **Mercutio.** This cannot anger him. 'Twould anger him
To raise a spirit in his mistress' circle
Of some strange nature, letting it there stand
Till she had laid it and conjured it down.
That were some spite; my invocation
30   Is fair and honest and in his mistress' name
I conjure only but to raise up him.

Benvolio. Come, he hath hid himself among these trees
To be consorted with the humorous night.
Blind is his love, and best befits the dark.

35 **Mercutio.** If love be blind, love cannot hit the mark.
Now will he sit under a medlar tree
And wish his mistress were that kind of fruit
As maids call medlars when they laugh alone.
Oh, Romeo, that she were, O, that she were
40   An open et cetera, thou a pop'rin pear!
Romeo, good night. I'll to my truckle bed;
This field-bed is too cold for me to sleep.
Come, shall we go?

Benvolio.   Go then, for 'tis in vain
45   To seek him here that means not to be found.

[Exeunt.]

1 **He jests:** Mercutio makes jokes. *What is Romeo saying about Mercutio?*

2-9 ***But soft . . . cast it off:*** Romeo sees Juliet at her window. For a moment he is speechless (***But soft:*** be still), but then he describes her beauty in glowing images of light and the heavenly bodies. He compares Juliet's beauty to the sun and says the moon looks sick and green because it is jealous of her.

11-14 ***O that . . . speaks:*** Romeo shifts back and forth between wanting to speak to Juliet and being afraid. *Why is he reluctant to let her know he is in the garden?*

15-22 ***Two of . . . not night:*** Romeo compares Juliet's eyes to stars in the sky.

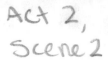

Scene 2 *Capulet's orchard.*

The following is one of the most famous scenes in all literature. The speeches contain some of the most beautiful poetry Shakespeare ever wrote.

Juliet appears on the balcony outside her room. She cannot see Romeo, who stands in the garden just below. At the beginning of the scene, both characters are speaking private thoughts to themselves. Romeo, however, can hear Juliet as she expresses her love for him despite his family name. Eventually, he speaks directly to her, and they declare their love for each other. Just before dawn Romeo leaves to make plans for their wedding.

[Enter Romeo.]

Romeo. He jests at scars that never felt a wound.

[Enter Juliet above at a window.]

But soft! What light through yonder window breaks?
It is the East, and Juliet is the sun!
Arise, fair sun, and kill the envious moon,
5 Who is already sick and pale with grief
That thou her maid art far more fair than she.
Be not her maid, since she is envious;
Her vestal livery is but sick and green,
And none but fools do wear it; cast it off.
10 It is my lady; O, it is my love!
O that she knew she were!
She speaks, yet she says nothing. What of that?
Her eye discourses; I will answer it.
I am too bold; 'tis not to me she speaks.
15 Two of the fairest stars in all the heaven,
Having some business, do entreat her eyes
To twinkle in their spheres till they return.
What if her eyes were there, they in her head?
The brightness of her cheek would shame those stars

26 Remember that Juliet does not know that Romeo is listening.

28-34 *thou art . . . of the air:* He compares Juliet to an angel *(winged messenger of heaven)* who stands over *(bestrides)* the clouds.

35-38 *wherefore:* why. Juliet asks why the man she loves is named Montague, a name that she is supposed to hate. *What does she ask him to do? What does she promise to do?*

46-52 Juliet tries to convince herself that a name is just a meaningless word that has nothing to do with the person. She asks Romeo to get rid of *(doff)* his name.

53-55 Romeo startles Juliet by speaking aloud.

20 As daylight doth a lamp; her eyes in heaven
   Would through the airy region stream so bright
   That birds would sing and think it were not night.
   See how she leans her cheek upon her hand!
   O that I were a glove upon that hand,
25 That I might touch that cheek!

Juliet.   Ay me!

Romeo. She speaks.
   O, speak again, bright angel! for thou art
   As glorious to this night, being o'er my head,
30 As is a winged messenger of heaven
   Unto the white-upturned wond'ring eyes
   Of mortals that fall back to gaze on him
   When he bestrides the lazy-pacing clouds
   And sails upon the bosom of the air.

35 **Juliet.** O Romeo, Romeo! wherefore art thou Romeo?
   Deny thy father and refuse thy name!
   Or, if thou wilt not, be but sworn my love,
   And I'll no longer be a Capulet.

Romeo. *[Aside]* Shall I hear more, or shall I speak at
40   this?

Juliet. 'Tis but thy name that is my enemy.
   Thou art thyself, though not a Montague.
   What's Montague? It is nor hand, nor foot,
   Nor arm, nor face, nor any other part
45 Belonging to a man. O, be some other name!
   What's in a name? That which we call a rose
   By any other name would smell as sweet.
   So Romeo would, were he not Romeo called,
   Retain that dear perfection which he owes
50 Without that title. Romeo, doff thy name;
   And for that name, which is no part of thee,
   Take all myself.

Romeo.   I take thee at thy word.
   Call me but love, and I'll be new baptized;

56-58 *How dare you, hiding **(bescreened),** listen to my private thoughts **(counsel)?***

68-69 ***How . . . wherefore:*** How did you get here, and why did you come?

73-78 ***With . . . thee:*** Love helped me climb **(o'erperch)** the walls. Neither walls nor your relatives are a hindrance **(let)** to my love. (Romeo is carried away with emotion, but Juliet is more realistic.) *What warning does she give?*

80-81 ***Look . . . enmity:*** Smile on me, and I will be defended against your family's hatred **(enmity).**

86-87 ***My life . . . love:*** I'd rather die from their hatred than have my death postponed **(prorogued)** if you don't love me.

55   Henceforth I never will be Romeo.

Juliet. What man art thou that, thus bescreened in
    night,
So stumblest on my counsel?

Romeo.   By a name
60   I know not how to tell thee who I am.
My name, dear saint, is hateful to myself,
Because it is an enemy to thee.
Had I it written, I would tear the word.

Juliet. My ears have yet not drunk a hundred words
65   Of that tongue's utterance, yet I know the sound.
Art thou not Romeo, and a Montague?

Romeo. Neither, fair saint, if either thee dislike.

Juliet. How camest thou hither, tell me, and
    wherefore?
70   The orchard walls are high and hard to climb,
And the place death, considering who thou art,
If any of my kinsmen find thee here.

Romeo. With love's light wings did I o'erperch these
    walls;
75   For stony limits cannot hold love out,
And what love can do, that dares love attempt.
Therefore thy kinsmen are no let to me.

Juliet. If they do see thee, they will murder thee.

Romeo. Alack, there lies more peril in thine eye
80   Than twenty of their swords! Look thou but sweet,
And I am proof against their enmity.

Juliet. I would not for the world they saw thee here.

Romeo. I have night's cloak to hide me from their
    sight;
85   And but thou love me, let them find me here.
My life were better ended by their hate
Than death prorogued, wanting of thy love.

94-98 ***Thou . . . compliment:*** Had I known you were listening, I would have gladly ***(fain)*** behaved more properly, but now it's too late for good manners ***(farewell compliment).*** *Why is Juliet embarrassed that Romeo overheard her?*

101-102 ***At . . . laughs:*** Jove (the king of the gods) laughs at lovers who lie to each other. *Why is Juliet worried?*

104-110 ***if . . . strange:*** You might think I've fallen in love too easily and that I am too forward. But I'll be truer to you than those who hide their feelings ***(be strange)*** and play romantic games.

118-120 ***swear . . . variable:*** *Why doesn't Juliet want Romeo to swear by the moon?*

Juliet. By whose direction foundst thou out this place?

Romeo. By love, that first did prompt me to enquire.
90   He lent me counsel, and I lent him eyes.
I am no pilot, yet, wert thou as far
As that vast shore washed with the farthest sea,
I would adventure for such merchandise.

Juliet. Thou knowest the mask of night is on my face;
95   Else would a maiden blush bepaint my cheek
For that which thou hast heard me speak tonight.
Fain would I dwell on form—fain, fain deny
What I have spoke; but farewell compliment!
Dost thou love me? I know thou wilt say "Ay";
100   And I will take thy word. Yet, if thou swearst,
Thou mayst prove false. At lovers' perjuries,
They say Jove laughs. O gentle Romeo,
If thou dost love, pronounce it faithfully.
Or if thou thinkst I am too quickly won,
105   I'll frown, and be perverse, and say thee nay,
So thou wilt woo; but else, not for the world.
In truth, fair Montague, I am too fond,
And therefore thou mayst think my 'havior light;
But trust me, gentleman, I'll prove more true
110   Than those that have more cunning to be strange.
I should have been more strange, I must confess,
But that thou overheardst, ere I was ware,
My true love's passion. Therefore pardon me,
And not impute this yielding to light love,
115   Which the dark night hath so discovered.

Romeo. Lady, by yonder blessed moon I swear,
That tips with silver all these fruit-tree tops—

Juliet. O, swear not by the moon, the inconstant
moon,
That monthly changes in her circled orb,
120   Lest that thy love prove likewise variable.

Romeo. What shall I swear by?

128-131 *I have . . . lightens:* Juliet is worried about their love *(contract),* which has happened as quickly as lightning and could be gone as fast. *What is Juliet's attitude at this point? Do you agree with her feelings about the relationship?*

150-151 *Anon:* Right away! Juliet calls to her nurse but meanwhile asks Romeo to wait till she returns. The Nurse's repeated calls begin to create urgency and tension.

Juliet.   Do not swear at all;
Or if thou wilt, swear by thy gracious self,
Which is the god of my idolatry,
125   And I'll believe thee.

Romeo.   If my heart's dear love—

Juliet. Well, do not swear. Although I joy in thee,
I have no joy of this contract tonight.
It is too rash, too unadvised, too sudden;
130   Too like the lightning, which doth cease to be
Ere one can say "It lightens." Sweet, good night!
This bud of love, by summer's ripening breath,
May prove a beauteous flow'r when next we meet.
Good night, good night! As sweet repose and rest
135   Come to thy heart as that within my breast!

Romeo. O, wilt thou leave me so unsatisfied?

Juliet. What satisfaction canst thou have tonight?

Romeo. The exchange of thy love's faithful vow for
mine.

140 **Juliet.** I gave thee mine before thou didst request it;
And yet I would it were to give again.

Romeo. Wouldst thou withdraw it? For what purpose,
love?

Juliet. But to be frank and give it thee again.
145   And yet I wish but for the thing I have.
My bounty is as boundless as the sea,
My love as deep; the more I give to thee,
The more I have, for both are infinite.
I hear some noise within. Dear love, adieu!

[Nurse calls within.]

150   Anon, good nurse! Sweet Montague, be true.
Stay but a little, I will come again.

[Exit.]

157-160 *If that . . . rite:* I'll send a messenger to you
tomorrow. If your intention is to marry me, tell the
messenger where and when the ceremony will be.
Although in love, Juliet continues to be practical and
wants proof that Romeo's intentions are serious.

173-174 *Love . . . looks:* The simile means that lovers meet as
eagerly as schoolboys leave their books; lovers separate
with the sadness of boys going to school.

175-181 *Hist . . . name:* Listen, Romeo, I wish I could speak
your name as loudly as a falconer calls his falcon
(tassel-gentle), but because of my parents, I must
whisper. Echo was a nymph in Greek mythology whose
unreturned love for Narcissus caused her to waste
away until only her voice was left.

Romeo. O blessed, blessed night! I am afeard,
Being in night, all this is but a dream,
Too flattering-sweet to be substantial.

[Re-enter Juliet, above.]

155 **Juliet.** Three words, dear Romeo, and good night
    indeed.
If that thy bent of love be honorable,
Thy purpose marriage, send me word tomorrow,
By one that I'll procure to come to thee,
160 Where and what time thou wilt perform the rite;
And all my fortunes at thy foot I'll lay
And follow thee my lord throughout the world.

Nurse. *[Within]* Madam!

Juliet. I come, anon.—But if thou meanst not well,
165 I do beseech thee—

Nurse. *[Within]*   Madam!

Juliet. By-and-by I come.—
To cease thy suit and leave me to my grief.
Tomorrow will I send.

170 **Romeo.**   So thrive my soul—

Juliet. A thousand times good night! *[Exit.]*

Romeo. A thousand times the worse, to want thy light!
Love goes toward love as schoolboys from their books;
But love from love, towards school with heavy looks.

[Enter Juliet again, above.]

175 **Juliet.** Hist! Romeo, hist! O for a falc'ner's voice
To lure this tassel-gentle back again!
Bondage is hoarse and may not speak aloud;
Else would I tear the cave where Echo lies,
And make her airy tongue more hoarse than mine
180 With repetition of my Romeo's name.
Romeo!

187-188 The ever-practical Juliet asks for details.

197-202 *I would . . . liberty:* I know you must go, but I want you close to me like a pet bird that a thoughtless child *(wanton)* keeps on a string.

Romeo. It is my soul that calls upon my name.
How silver-sweet sound lovers' tongues by night,
Like softest music to attending ears!

185 **Juliet.** Romeo!

Romeo.   My sweet?

Juliet. What o'clock tomorrow
Shall I send to thee?

Romeo.   By the hour of nine.

190 **Juliet.** I will not fail. 'Tis twenty years till then.
I have forgot why I did call thee back.

Romeo. Let me stand here till thou remember it.

Juliet. I shall forget, to have thee still stand there,
Rememb'ring how I love thy company.

195 **Romeo.** And I'll still stay, to have thee still forget,
Forgetting any other home but this.

Juliet. 'Tis almost morning. I would have thee gone—
And yet no farther than a wanton's bird,
That lets it hop a little from her hand,
200 Like a poor prisoner in his twisted gyves,
And with a silk thread plucks it back again,
So loving-jealous of his liberty.

Romeo. I would I were thy bird.

Juliet.   Sweet, so would I.
205 Yet I should kill thee with much cherishing.
Good night, good night! Parting is such sweet
    sorrow,
That I shall say good night till it be morrow.

[Exit.]

Romeo. Sleep dwell upon thine eyes, peace in thy
210   breast!
Would I were sleep and peace, so sweet to rest!

212-213 ***ghostly father:*** spiritual advisor or priest.
dear hap: good fortune.

1-31 Friar Laurence begins his speech by describing how
night changes into day. He then speaks of the herbs he
is collecting. The friar is particularly fascinated with the
idea that in herbs as well as man both good and evil
can exist.

5 Titan is the god whose chariot pulls the sun into the
sky each morning.

8 ***osier cage:*** willow basket.

10-11 ***The earth . . . womb:*** The same earth that acts as a
tomb, or burial ground, is also the womb, or
birthplace, of useful plants.

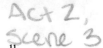

Hence will I to my ghostly father's cell,
His help to crave and my dear hap to tell.

[Exit.]

Scene 3 *Friar Laurence's cell in the monastery.*

*Romeo goes from Capulet's garden to the
monastery where Friar Laurence lives. The friar
knows Romeo well and often gives him advice.
As the scene begins, Friar Laurence is gathering
herbs in the early morning. He talks of good
and bad uses for herbs. Keep this in mind,
since Friar Laurence's skill at mixing herbs
becomes important later in the play. Romeo
tells the friar that he loves Juliet and wants to
marry her. The friar is amazed that Romeo has
forgotten about Rosaline so easily and suggests
that Romeo might be acting in haste. Eventually, however, he agrees to marry Romeo and
Juliet, hoping that the marriage might end the
feud between their families.*

[Enter Friar Laurence *alone, with a basket.]*

Friar Laurence. The grey-eyed morn smiles on the
    frowning night,
    Chequ'ring the Eastern clouds with streaks of light;
    And flecked darkness like a drunkard reels
5   From forth day's path and Titan's fiery wheels.
    Now, ere the sun advance his burning eye
    The day to cheer and night's dank dew to dry,
    I must upfill this osier cage of ours
    With baleful weeds and precious-juiced flowers.
10 The earth that's nature's mother is her tomb,
    What is her burying grave, that is her womb;
    And from her womb children of divers kind
    We sucking on her natural bosom find;
    Many for many virtues excellent,
15 None but for some, and yet all different.

The Tragedy of Romeo and Juliet   83

16-19 *mickle:* great. The Friar says that nothing from the earth is so evil that it doesn't do some good.

24-27 *Within . . . heart:* He holds a flower that can be used either as a poison or a medicine. If the flower is smelled, its fragrance can improve health in each part of the body; if eaten, it causes death.

29 *grace and rude will:* good and evil. Both exist in people as well as in plants.

33 *Benedicite* (bā' nā dē' chē ta'): God bless you.

35-44 *it argues . . . tonight:* Only a disturbed *(distempered)* mind could make you get up so early. Old people may have trouble sleeping, but it is not normal for someone as young as you. Or were you up all night?

46-47 *God . . . Rosaline:* The Friar is shocked that Romeo has not been to bed yet. *Where does he think Romeo has been?*

O, mickle is the powerful grace that lies
In plants, herbs, stones, and their true qualities;
For naught so vile that on the earth doth live
But to the earth some special good doth give;
20 Nor aught so good but, strained from that fair use,
Revolts from true birth, stumbling on abuse.
Virtue itself turns vice, being misapplied,
And vice sometime's by action dignified.
Within the infant rind of this small flower
25 Poison hath residence, and medicine power;
For this, being smelt, with that part cheers each part;
Being tasted, slays all senses with the heart.
Two such opposed kings encamp them still
In man as well as herbs—grace and rude will;
30 And where the worser is predominant,
Full soon the canker death eats up that plant.

[Enter Romeo.]

Romeo. Good morrow, father.

Friar Laurence.   Benedicite!
What early tongue so sweet saluteth me?
35 Young son, it argues a distempered head
So soon to bid good morrow to thy bed.
Care keeps his watch in every old man's eye,
And where care lodges sleep will never lie;
But where unbruised youth with unstuffed brain
40 Doth couch his limbs, there golden sleep doth reign.
Therefore thy earliness doth me assure
Thou art uproused with some distemp'rature;
Or if not so, then here I hit it right—
Our Romeo hath not been in bed tonight.

45 **Romeo.** That last is true, the sweeter rest was mine.

Friar Laurence. God pardon sin! Wast thou with
    Rosaline?

Romeo. With Rosaline, my ghostly father? No. I have
    forgot that name, and that name's woe.

52-61 Romeo tries to explain the situation and asks for help for both himself and his enemy (Juliet). In his excitement, Romeo talks in riddles, which confuse the Friar. The Friar tells Romeo to talk clearly.

73-74 *Young . . . eyes:* How would you paraphrase this sentence?

75-85 *brine:* salt water. The Friar is referring to the tears Romeo has been shedding for Rosaline. What is his opinion of Romeo's rapid change of affections from one girl to another?

Friar Laurence. That's my good son! But where hast
50   thou been then?

Romeo. I'll tell thee ere thou ask it me again.
    I have been feasting with mine enemy,
    Where on a sudden one hath wounded me
55   That's by me wounded. Both our remedies
    Within thy help and holy physic lies.
    I bear no hatred, blessed man, for, lo,
    My intercession likewise steads my foe.

Friar Laurence. Be plain, good son, and homely in thy
60   drift.
    Riddling confession finds but riddling shrift.

Romeo. Then plainly know my heart's dear love is set
    On the fair daughter of rich Capulet;
    As mine on hers, so hers is set on mine,
65   And all combined, save what thou must combine
    By holy marriage. When, and where, and how
    We met, we wooed, and made exchange of vow,
    I'll tell thee as we pass; but this I pray,
    That thou consent to marry us today.

70 **Friar Laurence.** Holy Saint Francis! What a change
     is here!
    Is Rosaline, that thou didst love so dear,
    So soon forsaken? Young men's love then lies
    Not truly in their hearts, but in their eyes.
75   Jesu Maria! What a deal of brine
    Hath washed thy sallow cheeks for Rosaline!
    How much salt water thrown away in waste,
    To season love, that of it doth not taste!
    The sun not yet thy sighs from heaven clears,
80   Thy old groans ring yet in mine ancient ears.
    Lo, here upon thy cheek the stain doth sit
    Of an old tear that is not washed off yet.
    If e'er thou wast thyself, and these woes thine,
    Thou and these woes were all for Rosaline.

86 *Women . . . men:* If men are so weak, women may be forgiven for sinning.

87-88 *chidst:* scolded. The Friar replies that he scolded Romeo for being lovesick, not for loving.

92-96 *She whom . . . spell:* Romeo says that the woman he loves feels the same way about him. That wasn't true of Rosaline. The Friar replies that Rosaline knew that he didn't know what real love is.

99-100 This marriage may work out well and turn the feud between your families into love.

102-103 *How is the Friar's warning similar to Juliet's fears in the previous scene?*

85 And art thou changed? Pronounce this sentence then:
Women may fall when there's no strength in men.

Romeo. Thou chidst me oft for loving Rosaline.

Friar Laurence. For doting, not for loving, pupil mine.

Romeo. And badest me bury love.

90 **Friar Laurence.**   Not in a grave
To lay one in, another ought to have.

Romeo. I pray thee chide not. She whom I love now
Doth grace for grace and love for love allow.
The other did not so.

95 **Friar Laurence.**   O, she knew well
Thy love did read by rote, that could not spell.
But come, young waverer, come go with me.
In one respect I'll thy assistant be;
For this alliance may so happy prove
100 To turn your households' rancor to pure love.

Romeo. O, let us hence! I stand on sudden haste.

Friar Laurence. Wisely, and slow. They stumble that
run fast.

[Exeunt.]

Scene 4 *A street.*

Several hours after his meeting with Friar Laurence, Romeo meets Benvolio and Mercutio in the street. He is excited and happy; his mood is key to the comic nature of this scene, which includes much talk of swordplay and many suggestive jokes. Mercutio makes fun of Tybalt and teases Romeo. The Nurse comes to carry a message from Romeo to Juliet. Romeo tells her that Juliet should meet him at Friar Laurence's cell for their secret marriage ceremony.

3 *man:* servant.

7-13 *Tybalt . . . dared:* The hot-headed Tybalt has sent a
letter to Romeo, challenging him to a duel. He is
obviously still angry about Romeo crashing the Capulet
party. Benvolio says that Romeo will do more than
answer the letter; he will accept Tybalt's challenge and
fight him.

17 *blind bow-boy's butt-shaft:* Cupid's dull practice
arrows; Mercutio suggests that Romeo fell in love with
very little work on Cupid's part.

20-27 *More than . . . hay:* Mercutio mocks Tybalt's name.
Prince of Cats refers to a cat in a fable named
"Tybalt" that was known for its slyness. Then Mercutio
makes fun of Tybalt's fancy new method of dueling,
comparing it to precision singing *(pricksong).*
Passado, punto, reverso, and *hay* were terms used
in the new dueling style.

29-37 *The pox . . . their bones:* As in his previous speech,
Mercutio makes fun of people, who like Tybalt, try to
impress everyone with their knowledge of the latest
fashions in dueling.

[Enter Benvolio and Mercutio.]

Mercutio. Where the devil should this Romeo be?
    Came he not home tonight?

Benvolio. Not to his father's. I spoke with his man.

Mercutio. Why, that same pale hard-hearted wench,
5   that Rosaline,
    Torments him so that he will sure run mad.

Benvolio. Tybalt, the kinsman to old Capulet,
    Hath sent a letter to his father's house.

Mercutio. A challenge, on my life.

10 **Benvolio.** Romeo will answer it.

Mercutio. Any man that can write may answer a letter.

Benvolio. Nay, he will answer the letter's master, how
    he dares, being dared.

Mercutio. Alas, poor Romeo, he is already dead!
15   stabbed with a white wench's black eye; shot through
    the ear with a love song; the very pin of his heart
    cleft with the blind bow-boy's butt-shaft; and is he
    a man to encounter Tybalt?

Benvolio. Why, what is Tybalt?

20 **Mercutio.** More than Prince of Cats, I can tell you. O,
    he's the courageous captain of compliments. He
    fights as you sing pricksong—keeps time, distance,
    and proportion; rests me his minim rest, one, two,
    and the third in your bosom! the very butcher of a
25   silk button, a duelist, a duelist! a gentleman of the
    very first house, of the first and second cause. Ah,
    the immortal *passado!* the *punto reverso!* the *hay!*

Benvolio. The what?

Mercutio. The pox of such antic, lisping, affecting
30   fantasticoes—these new tuners of accent! "By Jesu, a

39-45 *without his roe:* he is only part of himself. Mercutio
makes fun of Romeo's name and his lovesickness.
numbers: verses. Mercutio mentions Petrarch, who
wrote sonnets to his love, Laura. He then makes
insulting comments about famous lovers of the past.

46-51 *bon jour:* *(French)* good day. Here's a greeting to
match your fancy French trousers *(slop).* You did a
good job of getting away from us last night. (A piece
of counterfeit money was called a *slip.*)

51-97 In these lines, Romeo and Mercutio have a battle of
wits. They keep trying to top each other with funnier
comments and cleverer puns.

very good blade! a very tall man! a very good whore!" Why, is not this a lamentable thing, grandsire, that we should be thus afflicted with these strange flies, these fashion-mongers, these perdona-mi's, who stand so much on the new form that they cannot sit at ease on the old bench? O, their bones, their bones!

35

[Enter Romeo, no longer moody.]

Benvolio. Here comes Romeo! here comes Romeo!

Mercutio. Without his roe, like a dried herring. O,
40 flesh, flesh, how art thou fishified! Now is he for the numbers that Petrarch flowed in. Laura, to his lady, was but a kitchen wench (marry, she had a better love to berhyme her) Dido a dowdy, Cleopatra a gypsy, Helen and Hero hildings and harlots, Thisbe
45 a grey eye or so, but not to the purpose. Signior Romeo, *bon jour!* There's a French salutation to your French slop. You gave us the counterfeit fairly last night.

Romeo. Good morrow to you both. What counterfeit
50 did I give you?

Mercutio. The slip, sir, the slip. Can you not conceive?

Romeo. Pardon, good Mercutio. My business was great, and in such a case as mine a man may strain courtesy.

55 **Mercutio.** That's as much as to say, such a case as yours constrains a man to bow in the hams.

Romeo. Meaning, to curtsy.

Mercutio. Thou hast most kindly hit it.

Romeo. A most courteous exposition.

60 **Mercutio.** Nay, I am the very pink of courtesy.

Romeo. Pink for flower.

63 *pump:* shoe; ***well-flowered:*** shoes were "pinked," or punched out in flowerlike designs.

72-73 *Switch . . . match:* Keep going, or I'll claim victory.

77 *Was . . . goose?:* Have I proved that you are a foolish person *(goose)?*

86 *cheveril:* kid skin, which is flexible. Mercutio means that a little wit stretches a long way.

Mercutio. Right.

Romeo. Why, then is my pump well-flowered.

Mercutio. Well said! Follow me this jest now till thou
65   hast worn out thy pump, that, when the single sole
of it is worn, the jest may remain, after the wearing,
solely singular.

Romeo. Oh, single-soled jest, solely singular for the
singleness!

70 **Mercutio.** Come between us, good Benvolio! My wits
faint.

Romeo. Switch and spurs, switch and spurs! or I'll cry
a match.

Mercutio. Nay, if our wits run the wild-goose chase, I
75   am done; for thou hast more of the wild goose in
one of thy wits than, I am sure, I have in my whole
five. Was I with you there for the goose?

Romeo. Thou wast never with me for anything when
thou wast not there for the goose.

80 **Mercutio.** I will bite thee by the ear for that jest.

Romeo. Nay, good goose, bite not!

Mercutio. Thy wit is a very bitter sweeting; it is a most
sharp sauce.

Romeo. And is it not, then, well served in to a sweet
85 goose?

Mercutio. O, here's a wit of cheveril, that stretches
from an inch narrow to an ell broad!

Romeo. I stretch it out for that word "broad," which,
added to the goose, proves thee far and wide a
90 broad goose.

Mercutio. Why, is not this better now than groaning

95-97 *great natural:* an idiot like a jester or clown who carries a fool's stick *(bauble).* Mercutio is happy that Romeo is his old playful self again.

106-107 *Goodly gear:* something fine to joke about. A sail indicates that the Nurse in all her petticoats looks like a huge ship coming toward them.

110 *Anon:* Right away.

111 Fans were usually carried only by fine ladies. The Nurse is trying to pretend that she is more than a servant.

for love? Now art thou sociable, now art thou
Romeo;

95 now art thou what thou art, by art as well as by
nature. For this driveling love is like a great natural
that runs lolling up and down to hide his bauble in
a hole.

Benvolio. Stop there, stop there!

Mercutio. Thou desirest me to stop in my tale against
100 the hair.

Benvolio. Thou wouldst else have made thy tale large.

Mercutio. O, thou art deceived! I would have made it
short; for I was come to the whole depth of my tale,
and meant indeed to occupy the argument no
105 longer.

*[Enter Nurse and Peter, her servant. He is carrying a large
fan.]*

Romeo. Here's goodly gear!

Mercutio. A sail, a sail!

Benvolio. Two, two! a shirt and a smock.

Nurse. Peter!

110 **Peter.** Anon.

Nurse. My fan, Peter.

Mercutio. Good Peter, to hide her face; for her fan's
the fairer of the two.

Nurse. God ye good morrow, gentlemen.

115 **Mercutio.** God ye good-den, fair gentlewoman.

Nurse. Is it good-den?

Mercutio. 'Tis no less, I tell ye, for the bawdy hand of
the dial is now upon the prick of noon.

132-134 *confidence:* The Nurse means *conference,* she uses big words without understanding their meaning. Benvolio makes fun of this by using **endite** instead of *invite.*

135-145 Mercutio calls the Nurse a **bawd,** or woman who runs a house of prostitution. His song uses the insulting puns **hare,** a rabbit or a prostitute, and **hoar,** old.

Nurse. Out upon you! What a man are you!

120   **Romeo.** One, gentlewoman, that God hath made
himself to mar.

Nurse. By my troth, it is well said. "For himself to
mar," quoth'a? Gentlemen, can any of you tell me
where I may find the young Romeo?

125   **Romeo.** I can tell you; but young Romeo will be older
when you have found him than he was when you
sought him. I am the youngest of that name, for
fault of a worse.

Nurse. You say well.

130   **Mercutio.** Yea, is the worst well? Very well took, i'
faith! wisely, wisely.

Nurse. If you be he, sir, I desire some confidence with
you.

Benvolio. She will endite him to some supper.

135   **Mercutio.** A bawd, a bawd, a bawd! So ho!

Romeo. What hast thou found?

Mercutio. No hare, sir; unless a hare, sir, in a lenten
pie, that is something stale and hoar ere it be spent.

[Sings.]
      "An old hare hoar,
140   And an old hare hoar,
      Is very good meat in Lent.
      But a hare that is hoar,
      Is too much for a score
      When it hoars ere it be spent."
145   Romeo, will you come to your father's? We'll to
dinner thither.

Romeo. I will follow you.

Mercutio. Farewell, ancient lady. Farewell, *[sings]* lady,
lady, lady.

151 *ropery:* roguery, or jokes.

158-161 The Nurse is angry that Mercutio treated her like one of his loose women *(flirt-gills)* or his gangsterlike friends *(skainsmates).* She then complains that Peter did not come to her defense.

169-175 The Nurse warns Romeo that he'd better mean what he said about marrying Juliet. She holds back her own news to make sure that Romeo's love is genuine.

176 *commend me:* give my respectful greetings.

150 **Nurse.** Marry, farewell! I pray you, sir, what saucy
merchant was this that was so full of his ropery?

Romeo. A gentleman, nurse, that loves to hear himself
talk and will speak more in a minute than he will
stand to in a month.

155 **Nurse.** An 'a speak anything against me, I'll take him
down, an 'a were lustier than he is, and twenty such
Jacks; and if I cannot, I'll find those that shall.
Scurvy knave! I am none of his flirt-gills; I am none
of his skainsmates. *[Turning to* Peter.*]* And thou must
160 stand by too, and suffer every knave to use me at his
pleasure?

Peter. I saw no man use you at his pleasure. If I had,
my weapon should quickly have been out, I warrant
you. I dare draw as soon as another man, if I see
165 occasion in a good quarrel, and the law on my side.

Nurse. Now, afore God, I am so vexed that every part
about me quivers. Scurvy knave! Pray you, sir, a
word; and as I told you, my young lady bade me
enquire you out. What she bid me say, I will keep
170 to myself; but first let me tell ye, if ye should lead her
into a fool's paradise, as they say, it were a very gross
kind of behavior, as they say; for the gentlewoman
is young; and therefore, if you should deal double
with her, truly it were an ill thing to be offered to
175 any gentlewoman, and very weak dealing.

Romeo. Nurse, commend me to thy lady and mistress.
I protest unto thee—

Nurse. Good heart, and i' faith I will tell her as much.
Lord, Lord! she will be a joyful woman.

180 **Romeo.** What wilt thou tell her, nurse? Thou dost not
mark me.

184-187 Romeo tells the Nurse to have Juliet come to Friar Laurence's cell this afternoon using the excuse that she is going to confession *(shrift).* There she will receive forgiveness for her sins *(be shrived)* and be married.

193 *tackled stair:* a rope ladder. *topgallant:* highest point.

196-201 *quit thy pains:* reward you. The Nurse asks Romeo if his servant can be trusted and quotes the saying that two can keep a secret, but not three.

203-207 The Nurse, as is her way, begins to babble on and on. She mentions Paris' proposal but says Juliet would rather look at a toad than at Paris.

210-216 *clout . . . world:* old cloth in the entire world. *Doth not . . . hear it:* The Nurse tries to recall a clever saying that Juliet made up about Romeo and rosemary, the herb for remembrance, but she cannot remember it. She is sure that the two words couldn't begin with *R* because this letter sounds like a snarling dog. The Nurse mistakenly says *sententious* when she means *sentences.*

Nurse. I will tell her, sir, that you do protest, which, as
I take it, is a gentlemanlike offer.

Romeo. Bid her devise
185   Some means to come to shrift this afternoon;
And there she shall at Friar Laurence' cell
Be shrived and married. Here is for thy pains.

Nurse. No, truly, sir; not a penny.

Romeo. Go to! I say you shall.

190 **Nurse.** This afternoon, sir? Well, she shall be there.

Romeo. And stay, good nurse, behind the abbey wall.
Within this hour my man shall be with thee
And bring thee cords made like a tackled stair,
Which to the high topgallant of my joy
195   Must be my convoy in the secret night.
Farewell. Be trusty, and I'll quit thy pains.
Farewell. Commend me to thy mistress.

Nurse. Now God in heaven bless thee! Hark you, sir.

Romeo. What sayst thou, my dear nurse?

200 **Nurse.** Is your man secret? Did you ne'er hear say,
Two may keep counsel, putting one away?

Romeo. I warrant thee my man's as true as steel.

Nurse. Well, sir, my mistress is the sweetest lady. Lord,
Lord! when 'twas a little prating thing—O, there is a
205   nobleman in town, one Paris, that would fain lay
knife aboard; but she, good soul, had as lief see a
toad, a very toad, as see him. I anger her sometimes,
and tell her that Paris is the properer man; but
I'll warrant you, when I say so, she looks as pale as
210   any clout in the versal world. Doth not rosemary and
Romeo begin both with a letter?

Romeo. Ay, nurse, what of that? Both with an R.

220 *apace:* quickly.

4-6 *Love's . . . hills:* Love's messengers should be
thoughts, which travel ten times faster than sunbeams.

14 *bandy:* toss.

Nurse. Ah, mocker! that's the dog's name. R is for
    the—No; I know it begins with some other letter;
215 and she hath the prettiest sententious of it, of you
    and rosemary, that it would do you good to hear it.

Romeo. Commend me to thy lady.

Nurse. Ay, a thousand times. *[Exit* Romeo.*]* Peter!

Peter. Anon.

220 **Nurse.** Peter, take my fan, and go before, and apace.

    [Exeunt.]

Scene 5 *Capulet's orchard.*

> *Juliet is a nervous wreck, having waited for
> more than three hours for the Nurse to return.
> When the Nurse does arrive, she simply can't
> come to the point. Juliet gets more and more
> upset, until the Nurse finally reveals the
> wedding arrangements.*

[Enter Juliet.*]*

Juliet. The clock struck nine when I did send the
    nurse;
    In half an hour she promised to return.
    Perchance she cannot meet him. That's not so.
    O, she is lame! Love's heralds should be thoughts,
5   Which ten times faster glide than the sun's beams
    Driving back shadows over lowering hills.
    Therefore do nimble-pinioned doves draw Love,
    And therefore hath the wind-swift Cupid wings.
    Now is the sun upon the highmost hill
10 Of this day's journey, and from nine till twelve
    Is three long hours; yet she is not come.
    Had she affections and warm youthful blood,
    She would be as swift in motion as a ball;
    My words would bandy her to my sweet love,

16 *feign as:* act as if.

21-22 The Nurse teases Juliet by putting on a sad face as if the news were bad.

26-27 *give me . . . I had:* Leave me alone for a while. I ache all over because of the running back and forth I've been doing.

39-40 *Say . . . bad:* Tell me if the news is good or bad, and I'll wait for the details.

41 *simple:* foolish.

15   And his to me.
        But old folks, many feign as they were dead—
        Unwieldy, slow, heavy, and pale as lead.

        [Enter Nurse and Peter.]

        O God, she comes! O honey nurse, what news?
        Hast thou met with him? Send thy man away.

20   **Nurse.** Peter, stay at the gate.

        [Exit Peter.]

        Juliet. Now, good sweet nurse—O Lord, why lookst
            thou sad?
        Though news be sad, yet tell them merrily;
        If good, thou shamest the music of sweet news
25   By playing it to me with so sour a face.

        Nurse. I am aweary, give me leave awhile.
        Fie, how my bones ache! What a jaunce have I had!

        Juliet. I would thou hadst my bones, and I thy news.
        Nay, come, I pray thee speak. Good, good nurse,
30   speak.

        Nurse. Jesu, what haste! Can you not stay awhile?
        Do you not see that I am out of breath?

        Juliet. How art thou out of breath when thou hast
            breath
35   To say to me that thou art out of breath?
        The excuse that thou dost make in this delay
        Is longer than the tale thou dost excuse.
        Is thy news good or bad? Answer to that.
        Say either, and I'll stay the circumstance.
40   Let me be satisfied, is't good or bad?

        Nurse. Well, you have made a simple choice; you know
        not how to choose a man. Romeo? No, not he.
        Though his face be better than any man's, yet his leg
        excels all men's; and for a hand and a foot, and a
45   body, though they be not to be talked on, yet they

        The Tragedy of Romeo and Juliet   107

55-56 ***Beshrew . . . down:*** Curse you for making me endanger my health by running around. *Considering the Nurse's feelings for Juliet, is this really an angry curse?*

66-69 ***O God's . . . yourself:*** Are you so eager? Control yourself *(come up).* Is this the treatment I get for my pain? From now on, run your own errands.

70 ***coil:*** fuss.

71-73 ***Have you . . . cell:*** Do you have permission to go to confession today? Then go quickly to Friar Laurence's cell, where Romeo wants to marry you.

77-79 The Nurse will get the ladder that Romeo will use to climb to Juliet's room after they are married.

are past compare. He is not the flower of courtesy,
but, I'll warrant him, as gentle as a lamb. Go thy
ways, wench; serve God. What, have you dined at
home?

50 **Juliet.** No, no. But all this did I know before.
What say he of our marriage? What of that?

Nurse. Lord, how my head aches! What a head have I!
It beats as it would fall in twenty pieces.
My back o' t' other side—ah, my back, my back!
55 Beshrew your heart for sending me about
To catch my death with jauncing up and down!

Juliet. I' faith, I am sorry that thou art not well.
Sweet, sweet, sweet nurse, tell me, what says my love?

Nurse. Your love says, like an honest gentleman, and a
60 courteous, and a kind, and a handsome, and, I
warrant, a virtuous—Where is your mother?

Juliet. Where is my mother? Why, she is within.
Where should she be? How oddly thou repliest!
"Your love says, like an honest gentleman,
65 'Where is your mother?'"

Nurse.   O God's Lady dear!
Are you so hot? Marry come up, I trow.
Is this the poultice for my aching bones?
Henceforward do your messages yourself.

70 **Juliet.** Here's such a coil! Come, what says Romeo?

Nurse. Have you got leave to go to shrift today?

Juliet. I have.

Nurse. Then hie you hence to Friar Laurence' cell;
There stays a husband to make you a wife.
75 Now comes the wanton blood up in your cheeks:
They'll be in scarlet straight at any news.
Hie you to church; I must another way,
To fetch a ladder, by the which your love

1-2 *So smile . . . us not:* May heaven bless this act and not blame us for it in the future *(after-hours).*

3-8 *come what . . . mine:* No future sorrow can outweigh *(countervail)* the joy Juliet brings me. Once we're married, I don't even care if I die.

9-16 *These . . . slow:* The Friar compares Romeo's passion to gunpowder and the fire that ignites it: both are destroyed; then to honey, whose sweetness can destroy the appetite. He reminds Romeo to practice moderation in love. *How likely is it that Romeo will follow this advice?*

19-21 *A lover . . . vanity:* A lover can walk across a spider's web *(gossamer),* almost like walking on air.

Must climb a bird's nest soon when it is dark.
80 I am the drudge, and toil in your delight;
But you shall bear the burden soon at night.
Go; I'll to dinner; hie you to the cell.

Juliet. Hie to high fortune! Honest nurse, farewell.

[Exeunt.]

Scene 6 *Friar Laurence's cell.*

Friar Laurence cautions Romeo to be more sensible in his love for Juliet. When she arrives, the two confess their love to each other and prepare to be married by Friar Laurence.

[Enter Friar Laurence and Romeo.]

Friar Laurence. So smile the heavens upon this holy act
That after-hours with sorrow chide us not!

Romeo. Amen, amen! But come what sorrow can,
It cannot countervail the exchange of joy
5   That one short minute gives me in her sight.
Do thou but close our hands with holy words,
Then love-devouring death do what he dare—
It is enough I may but call her mine.

Friar Laurence. These violent delights have violent
10   ends
And in their triumph die, like fire and powder,
Which, as they kiss, consume. The sweetest honey
Is loathsome in his own deliciousness
And in the taste confounds the appetite.
15   Therefore love moderately: long love doth so;
Too swift arrives as tardy as too slow.

[Enter Juliet.]

Here comes the lady. O, so light a foot
Will ne'er wear out the everlasting flint.
A lover may bestride the gossamer

22 *ghostly confessor:* spiritual advisor.

25 *As much to him:* The same greeting to Romeo that he offers to me.

26-31 If you are as happy as I am and have more skill to proclaim it, then sweeten the air by singing of our happiness to the world.

32-33 *Conceit . . . ornament:* True understanding *(conceit)* needs no words.

39-40 *you shall . . . one:* Until I have performed the wedding ceremony, I will not allow you to be alone together.

20   That idles in the wanton summer air,
      And yet not fall; so light is vanity.

Juliet. Good even to my ghostly confessor.

Friar Laurence. Romeo shall thank thee, daughter, for
      us both.

25 **Juliet.** As much to him, else is his thanks too much.

Romeo. Ah, Juliet, if the measure of thy joy
      Be heaped like mine, and that thy skill be more
      To blazon it, then sweeten with thy breath
      This neighbor air, and let rich music's tongue
30   Unfold the imagined happiness that both
      Receive in either by this dear encounter.

Juliet. Conceit, more rich in matter than in words,
      Brags of his substance, not of ornament.
      They are but beggars that can count their worth;
35   But my true love is grown to such excess
      I cannot sum up sum of half my wealth.

Friar Laurence. Come, come with me, and we will
      make short work;
      For, by your leaves, you shall not stay alone
40   Till Holy Church incorporate two in one.

[Exeunt.]

3-4 ***we shall . . . stirring:*** We shall not avoid a fight since the heat makes people angry.

8-9 ***by the . . . drawer:*** feeling the effects of a second drink, is ready to fight ***(draw on)*** the waiter who's pouring drinks ***(drawer).***

13-14 ***as soon moved . . . to be moved:*** as likely to get angry and start a fight.

ACT THREE

Scene 1 *A public place.*

*Act Two ended with the joyful Romeo and
Juliet secretly married. Their happiness,
however, is about to end abruptly. In this
scene, Mercutio, Benvolio, and Romeo meet
Tybalt on the street. Tybalt insults Romeo, but
Romeo, who has just returned from his
wedding, remains calm. Mercutio, on the
other hand, is furious with Tybalt, and they
begin to fight. As Romeo tries to separate
them, Tybalt stabs Mercutio, who later dies.
Romeo then challenges Tybalt, kills him, and
flees. The Prince arrives and demands an
explanation. He announces that Romeo will be
killed if he does not leave Verona immediately.*

[Enter Mercutio, Benvolio, Page and Servants.]

Benvolio. I pray thee, good Mercutio, let's retire.
The day is hot, the Capulets abroad,
And if we meet, we shall not scape a brawl,
For now, these hot days, is the mad blood stirring.

5 **Mercutio.** Thou art like one of those fellows that, when
he enters the confines of a tavern, claps me his
sword upon the table and says "God send me no
need of thee!" and by the operation of the second
cup draws him on the drawer, when indeed there is
10 no need.

Benvolio. Am I like such a fellow?

Mercutio. Come, come, thou art as hot a Jack in thy
mood as any in Italy; and as soon moved to be

16-31 Picture Mercutio and Benvolio playfully roughing each other up as this conversation proceeds. Mercutio teases his friend by insisting that Benvolio is quick to pick a fight. However, everyone knows that Benvolio is gentle and peace loving. Mercutio could have been describing himself.

29-30 *doublet:* jacket. *ribend:* ribbon or laces.

32-34 *An I . . . quarter:* If I picked fights as quickly as you do, anybody could own me for the smallest amount of money.

36 *What do you predict will happen now that Tybalt has appeared?*

38-57 As you read this exchange, ask yourself, *Who is responsible for starting this fight?*

41-44 Mercutio dares Tybalt to add a punch *(blow)* to whatever he has to say. Tybalt says he'll do so if Mercutio gives him an excuse.

moody, and as soon moody to be moved.

15 **Benvolio.** And what to?

Mercutio. Nay an there were two such, we should have
none shortly, for one would kill the other. Thou!
why, thou wilt quarrel with a man that hath a hair
more or a hair less in his beard than thou hast. Thou
20 wilt quarrel with a man for cracking nuts, having no
other reason but because thou hast hazel eyes. What
eye but such an eye would spy out such a quarrel?
Thy head is as full of quarrels as an egg is full of
meat; and yet thy head hath been beaten as addle as
25 an egg for quarreling. Thou hast quarreled with a
man for coughing in the street, because he hath
wakened thy dog that hath lain asleep in the sun.
Didst thou not fall out with a tailor for wearing his
new doublet before Easter? with another for tying
30 his new shoes with old riband? And yet thou wilt
tutor me from quarreling!

Benvolio. An I were so apt to quarrel as thou art, any
man should buy the fee simple of my life for an
hour and a quarter.

35 **Mercutio.** The fee simple? O simple!

[Enter Tybalt *and others.]*

Benvolio. By my head, here come the Capulets.

Mercutio. By my heel, I care not.

Tybalt. Follow me close, for I will speak to them.
Gentlemen, good den. A word with one of you.

40 **Mercutio.** And but one word with one of us?
Couple it with something; make it a word and a
blow.

Tybalt. You shall find me apt enough to that, sir, an
you will give me occasion.

47-51 *consortest:* keep company with. Tybalt means "You are friendly with Romeo." Mercutio pretends to misunderstand him, assuming that Tybalt is insulting him by calling Romeo and himself a **consort,** a group of traveling musicians. He then refers to his sword as his **fiddlestick,** the bow for a fiddle.

52-55 Benvolio steps between Tybalt and Mercutio, trying to keep peace between them. *What does he suggest they do?*

58-61 When Romeo enters, Mercutio again pretends to misunderstand Tybalt. By **my man,** Tybalt means "the man I'm looking for." Mercutio takes it to mean "my servant." (**Livery** is a servant's uniform.) He assures Tybalt that the only place Romeo would follow him as a servant is to the dueling field.

65-68 I forgive your anger because I have reason to love you. *What reason is Romeo referring to? Who else knows about this reason?*

69 *Boy:* an insulting term of address to Romeo.

74 *tender:* cherish.

Mercutio. Could you not take some occasion without
giving? ₄₅

Tybalt. Mercutio, thou consortest with Romeo.

Mercutio. Consort? What, dost thou make us minstrels?
An thou make minstrels of us, look to hear nothing
but discords. Here's my fiddlestick; here's that shall
make you dance. Zounds, consort!

Benvolio. We talk here in the public haunt of men.
Either withdraw unto some private place
And reason coldly of your grievances,
Or else depart. Here all eyes gaze on us.

Mercutio. Men's eyes were made to look, and let them
gaze. I will not budge for no man's pleasure, I.

[Enter Romeo.]

Tybalt. Well, peace be with you, sir. Here comes my
man.

Mercutio. But I'll be hanged, sir, if he wear your livery.
Marry, go before to field, he'll be your follower!
Your worship in that sense may call him man.

Tybalt. Romeo, the love I bear thee can afford
No better term than this: thou art a villain.

Romeo. Tybalt, the reason that I have to love thee
Doth much excuse the appertaining rage
To such a greeting. Villain am I none.
Therefore farewell. I see thou knowst me not.

Tybalt. Boy, this shall not excuse the injuries
That thou hast done me; therefore turn and draw.

Romeo. I do protest I never injured thee,
But love thee better than thou canst devise
Till thou shalt know the reason of my love;
And so, good Capulet, which name I tender
As dearly as mine own, be satisfied.

76-78 Mercutio is disgusted by Romeo's calm response to Tybalt and assumes that Romeo is afraid to fight. *Alla stoccata* is a move used in sword fighting. Mercutio calls Tybalt a *ratcatcher,* an insult based on Tybalt's name. Then he dares him to step aside and fight *(walk).*

81-83 *I mean . . . eight:* I intend to take one of your nine lives (as a cat has) and give a beating to the other eight.

88 Be on your guard; I'm about to attack. (A *passado* is a move used in sword fighting.)

89-93 Imagine a sword fight between Tybalt and Mercutio. Romeo, off to the side with Benvolio, is frantic at what is happening. He wants desperately to stop this fighting *(bandying)* between his friend and his new in-law. He steps between the duellers and manages to hold Mercutio, but Tybalt stabs Mercutio under Romeo's arm.

95 *A plague . . . sped:* I curse both the Montagues and the Capulets. I am destroyed.

Mercutio. O calm, dishonorable, vile submission!
Alla stoccata carries it away.

[Draws.]

Tybalt, you ratcatcher, will you walk?

Tybalt. What wouldst thou have with me?

80 **Mercutio.** Good King of Cats, nothing but one of your
nine lives. That I mean to make bold withal, and, as
you shall use me hereafter, dry-beat the rest of the
eight. Will you pluck your sword out of his pilcher
by the ears? Make haste, lest mine be about your ears
85 ere it be out.

Tybalt. I am for you.

[Draws.]

Romeo. Gentle Mercutio, put thy rapier up.

Mercutio. Come, sir, your *passado!*

[They fight.]

Romeo. Draw, Benvolio; beat down their weapons.
90 Gentlemen, for shame! forbear this outrage!
Tybalt, Mercutio, the Prince expressly hath
Forbid this bandying in Verona streets.
Hold, Tybalt! Good Mercutio!

*[Tybalt, under Romeo's arm, thrusts Mercutio in, and flies
with his Men.]*

Mercutio. I am hurt.
95 A plague o' both your houses! I am sped.
Is he gone and hath nothing?

Benvolio.   What, art thou hurt?

Mercutio. Ay, ay, a scratch, a scratch. Marry, 'tis
enough.
100 Where is my page? Go, villain, fetch a surgeon.

[Exit Page.]

102-110 Picture Mercutio lying on the ground, bleeding, surrounded by horrified friends. Even as he is dying, he continues to joke and to make nasty remarks about Tybalt. He makes a pun on the word *grave.*

116-122 My true friend is dying because of me. My reputation has been damaged by a man who has been my relative for only an hour. My love for Juliet has made me less manly and brave.

124 *aspired:* soared to.

126-127 This awful day will be followed by more of the same.

129-136 Romeo sees Tybalt still living, while Mercutio lies dead. *What challenge does Romeo make to Tybalt?*

Romeo. Courage, man. The hurt cannot be much.

Mercutio. No, 'tis not so deep as a well, nor so wide as
a church door; but 'tis enough, 'twill serve. Ask for
me tomorrow, and you shall find me a grave man. I
105   am peppered, I warrant, for this world. A plague o'
both your houses! Zounds, a dog, a rat, a mouse, a
cat, to scratch a man to death! A braggart, a rogue, a
villain, that fights by the book of arithmetic! Why the
devil came you between us? I was hurt under your
110   arm.

Romeo. I thought all for the best.

Mercutio. Help me into some house, Benvolio,
Or I shall faint. A plague o' both your houses!
They have made worms' meat of me. I have it,
115   And soundly too. Your houses!

[Exit, supported by Benvolio.]

Romeo. This gentleman, the Prince's near ally,
My very friend, hath got this mortal hurt
In my behalf—my reputation stained
With Tybalt's slander—Tybalt, that an hour
120   Hath been my kinsman, O sweet Juliet,
Thy beauty hath made me effeminate
And in my temper softened valor's steel!

[Re-enter Benvolio.]

Benvolio. O Romeo, Romeo, brave Mercutio's dead!
That gallant spirit hath aspired the clouds,
125   Which too untimely here did scorn the earth.

Romeo. This day's black fate on mo days doth depend;
This but begins the woe others must end.

[Re-enter Tybalt.]

Benvolio. Here comes the furious Tybalt back again.

Romeo. Alive in triumph, and Mercutio slain?

140 Imagine the sword fight between the two men, which probably goes on for several minutes. The fight ends with Romeo running his sword through Tybalt.

141-144 Don't just stand there! The Prince will sentence you to death if he catches you.

145 *I am fortune's fool:* Fate has made a fool of me.

153-154 Benvolio says he can tell *(discover)* what happened.

130 Away to heaven respective lenity,
And fire-eyed fury be my conduct now!
Now, Tybalt, take the "villain" back again
That late thou gavest me, for Mercutio's soul
Is but a little way above our heads,
135 Staying for thine to keep him company.
Either thou or I, or both, must go with him.

Tybalt. Thou, wretched boy, that didst consort him
    here,
Shalt with him hence.

140 **Romeo.**   This shall determine that.

[They fight. Tybalt falls.]

Benvolio. Romeo, away, be gone!
The citizens are up, and Tybalt slain.
Stand not amazed. The Prince will doom thee death
If thou art taken. Hence, be gone, away!

145 **Romeo.** O, I am fortune's fool!

Benvolio.   Why dost thou stay?

[Exit Romeo.]

[Enter Citizens.]

Citizen. Which way ran he that killed Mercutio?
Tybalt, that murderer, which way ran he?

Benvolio. There lies that Tybalt.

150 **Citizen.**   Up, sir, go with me.
I charge thee in the Prince's name obey.

[Enter Prince with his Attendants, Montague, Capulet,
their Wives, and others.]

Prince. Where are the vile beginners of this fray?

Benvolio. O noble Prince, I can discover all
The unlucky manage of this fatal brawl.

160-161 *as thou . . . Montague:* If your word is good, you will sentence Romeo to death for killing a Capulet.

164-190 Benvolio explains what has just happened. *How accurate is his retelling?*

166-167 *Romeo, that . . . was:* Romeo talked calmly *(fair)* and told Tybalt to think how trivial *(nice)* the argument was.

171-172 *Could . . . peace:* All this could not quiet Tybalt's anger; he would not listen to pleas for peace.

181-182 *His agile . . . rushes:* He rushed between them and pushed down their swords.

186 *entertained:* thought of.

155 There lies the man, slain by young Romeo,
That slew thy kinsman, brave Mercutio.

Lady Capulet. Tybalt, my cousin! O my brother's child!
O Prince! O cousin! O husband! O, the blood is
spilled
160 Of my dear kinsman! Prince, as thou art true,
For blood of ours shed blood of Montague.
O cousin, cousin!

Prince. Benvolio, who began this bloody fray?

Benvolio. Tybalt, here slain, whom Romeo's hand did
165 slay.
Romeo, that spoke him fair, bid him bethink
How nice the quarrel was, and urged withal
Your high displeasure. All this—uttered
With gentle breath, calm look, knees humbly
170 bowed—
Could not take truce with the unruly spleen
Of Tybalt deaf to peace, but that he tilts
With piercing steel at bold Mercutio's breast;
Who, all as hot, turns deadly point to point,
175 And, with a martial scorn, with one hand beats
Cold death aside and with the other sends
It back to Tybalt, whose dexterity
Retorts it. Romeo he cries aloud,
"Hold, friends! friends, part!" and swifter than his
180 tongue,
His agile arm beats down their fatal points,
And 'twixt them rushes; underneath whose arm
An envious thrust from Tybalt hit the life
Of stout Mercutio, and then Tybalt fled,
185 But by-and-by comes back to Romeo,
Who had but newly entertained revenge,
And to't they go like lightning; for, ere I
Could draw to part them, was stout Tybalt slain;
And, as he fell, did Romeo turn and fly.
190 This is the truth, or let Benvolio die.

191-192   *Why does Lady Capulet think Benvolio is lying? What wild accusation does she go on to make?*

201-202   Romeo is guilty only of avenging Mercutio's death, which the law would have done anyway.

204-215   The Prince banishes Romeo from Verona. He angrily points out that one of his own relatives, Mercutio, is now dead because of the feud. The Prince promises that if Romeo does not leave Verona immediately, he will be put to death.

Lady Capulet. He is a kinsman to the Montague;
Affection makes him false, he speaks not true.
Some twenty of them fought in this black strife,
And all those twenty could but kill one life.
195   I beg for justice, which thou, Prince, must give.
Romeo slew Tybalt; Romeo must not live.

Prince. Romeo slew him; he slew Mercutio.
Who now the price of his dear blood doth owe?

Montague. Not Romeo, Prince; he was Mercutio's
200   friend;
His fault concludes but what the law should end,
The life of Tybalt.

Prince.   And for that offense
Immediately we do exile him hence.
205   I have an interest in your hate's proceeding,
My blood for your rude brawls doth lie a-bleeding;
But I'll amerce you with so strong a fine
That you shall all repent the loss of mine.
I will be deaf to pleading and excuses;
210   Nor tears nor prayers shall purchase out abuses.
Therefore use none. Let Romeo hence in haste,
Else, when he is found, that hour is his last.
Bear hence this body, and attend our will.
Mercy but murders, pardoning those that kill.

     [Exeunt.]

Scene 2 *Capulet's orchard.*

*The scene begins with Juliet impatiently
waiting for night to come so that Romeo can
climb to her bedroom on the rope ladder.
Suddenly the Nurse enters with the terrible
news of Tybalt's death and Romeo's
banishment. Juliet mourns for the loss of her
cousin and her husband and threatens to kill
herself. To calm her, the Nurse promises to
find Romeo and bring him to Juliet before he
leaves Verona.*

The Tragedy of Romeo and Juliet   129

1-4 Juliet is wishing for nightfall, when Romeo is to come to her room. **Phoebus** is the god whose chariot pulls the sun across the sky; **Phaeton** was his son, who lost control of the chariot when he drove it too fast.

14-16 **Hood . . . modesty:** Juliet asks that the darkness hide her blushing cheeks on her wedding night.

22-26 *What does Juliet think should happen to Romeo after he dies?*

27-32 **I have . . . wear them:** Juliet protests that she has gone through the wedding ceremony **(bought the mansion)** but is still waiting to enjoy the rewards of marriage. She then compares herself to an excited, impatient child on the night before a holiday or festival.

[Enter Juliet *alone.]*

Juliet. Gallop apace, you fiery-footed steeds,
    Toward Phoebus' lodging! Such a wagoner
    As Phaëton would whip you to the West,
    And bring in cloudy night immediately.
5   Spread thy close curtain, love-performing night,
    That runaways' eyes may wink, and Romeo
    Leap to these arms, untalked of and unseen.
    Lovers can see to do their amorous rites
    By their own beauties; or, if love be blind,
10   It best agrees with night. Come, civil night,
    Thou sober-suited matron, all in black,
    And learn me how to lose a winning match,
    Played for a pair of stainless maidenhoods.
    Hood my unmanned blood bating in my cheeks.
15   With thy black mantle; till strange love, grown bold,
    Think true love acted simple modesty.
    Come, night; come, Romeo, come; thou day in night;
    For thou wilt lie upon the wings of night
    Whiter than new snow on a raven's back.
20   Come, gentle night; come, loving, black-browed
       night;
    Give me my Romeo; and, when he shall die,
    Take him and cut him out in little stars,
    And he will make the face of heaven so fine
25   That all the world will be in love with night
    And pay no worship to the garish sun.
    O, I have bought the mansion of a love,
    But not possessed it; and though I am sold,
    Not yet enjoyed. So tedious is this day
30   As is the night before some festival
    To an impatient child that hath new robes
    And may not wear them. Oh, here comes my
       nurse,

[Enter Nurse, *wringing her hands, with the ladder of
cords in her lap.]*

36-37 ***cords . . . fetch:*** the rope ladder Romeo told you to get.

41-47 ***well-a-day:*** an expression used when someone has bad news. The Nurse wails and moans without clearly explaining what has happened. Juliet misunderstands and assumes that Romeo is dead.

50-55 Juliet's *I* means "aye," or yes. She is in agony, thinking Romeo dead, and begs the Nurse to answer clearly. A ***cockatrice*** is a mythological beast whose glance killed its victims.

58-61 ***God . . . mark:*** an expression meant to scare off evil powers, similar to "Knock on wood." The Nurse says she saw the corpse ***(corse)***, covered ***(bedaubed)*** in blood and gore. She fainted ***(swounded)*** at the sight of it.

62-66 Juliet says her heart is broken and bankrupt ***(bankrout).*** She wants to be buried with Romeo, or share his casket ***(bier).***

And she brings news; and every tongue that speaks
But Romeo's name speaks heavenly eloquence.

35   Now, nurse, what news? What hast thou there?
     the cords
That Romeo bid thee fetch?

Nurse.   Ay, ay, the cords.

Juliet. Ay me! what news? Why dost thou wring thy
40   hands?

Nurse. Ah, well-a-day! he's dead, he's dead, he's dead!
We are undone, lady, we are undone!
Alack the day! he's gone, he's killed, he's dead!

Juliet. Can heaven be so envious?

45 **Nurse.**   Romeo can,
Though heaven cannot. O Romeo, Romeo!
Who ever would have thought it? Romeo!

Juliet. What devil art thou that dost torment me thus?
This torture should be roared in dismal hell.
50   Hath Romeo slain himself? Say thou but "I,"
And that bare vowel "I" shall poison more
Than the death-darting eye of a cockatrice.
I am not I, if there be such an "I,"
Or those eyes shut, that make thee answer "I."
55   If he be slain, say "I," or if not, "no."
Brief sounds determine of my weal or woe.

Nurse. I saw the wound, I saw it with mine eyes,
(God save the mark!) here on his manly breast.
A piteous corse, a bloody piteous corse;
60   Pale, pale as ashes, all bedaubed in blood,
All in gore blood. I swounded at the sight.

Juliet. O, break, my heart! poor bankrout, break
     at once!
To prison, eyes; ne'er look on liberty!
65   Vile earth, to earth resign; end motion here,
And thou and Romeo press one heavy bier!

70-74 Juliet is trying to make sense of what the Nurse has said.

79-91 In her grief Juliet cries out a series of contradictory phrases, which show her conflicting feelings. A **fiend** is a demon. *How are* **fiend angelical** *and* **dove-feathered raven** *contradictory? What is Juliet's first reaction to the news that Romeo killed Tybalt?*

92-94 *There's . . . dissemblers:* All men are liars and pretenders.

95 *where's . . . vitae:* Where's my servant? Give me some brandy.

98-103 *Blistered . . . him:* Juliet has now recovered a bit from the shock of the news. *How does she respond to the Nurse's wish that shame come to Romeo?*

Nurse. O Tybalt, Tybalt, the best friend I had!
O courteous Tybalt! honest gentleman!
That ever I should live to see thee dead!

70 **Juliet.** What storm is this that blows so contrary?
Is Romeo slaughtered, and is Tybalt dead?
My dear-loved cousin, and my dearer lord?
Then, dreadful trumpet, sound the general doom!
For who is living, if those two are gone?

75 **Nurse.** Tybalt is gone, and Romeo banished;
Romeo that killed him, he is banished.

Juliet. O God! Did Romeo's hand shed Tybalt's blood?

Nurse. It did! it did! alas the day, it did!

Juliet. O serpent heart, hid with a flow'ring face!
80 Did ever dragon keep so fair a cave?
Beautiful tyrant! fiend angelical!
Dove-feathered raven! wolvish-ravening lamb!
Despised substance of divinest show!
Just opposite to what thou justly seemst,
85 A damned saint, an honorable villain!
O nature, what hadst thou to do in hell
When thou didst bower the spirit of a fiend
In mortal paradise of such sweet flesh?
Was ever book containing such vile matter
90 So fairly bound? O, that deceit should dwell
In such a gorgeous palace!

Nurse.   There's no trust,
No faith, no honesty in men; all perjured,
All forsworn, all naught, all dissemblers.
95 Ah, where's my man? Give me some aqua vitae.
These griefs, these woes, these sorrows make me old.
Shame come to Romeo!

Juliet.   Blistered be thy tongue
For such a wish! He was not born to shame.
100 Upon his brow shame is ashamed to sit;

106-117 ***Shall . . . husband:*** Juliet is in turmoil. She is ashamed that she criticized her husband. She realizes that if he hadn't killed Tybalt, Tybalt would have killed him.

119-125 *What is Juliet wishing she hadn't heard?*

125-137 Juliet says that if the news of Tybalt's death had been followed by the news of her parents' deaths, she would have felt normal ***(modern),*** or expected, grief. To follow the story of Tybalt's death with the terrible news of Romeo's banishment creates a sorrow so deep it cannot be expressed in words.

For 'tis a throne where honor may be crowned
Sole monarch of the universal earth.
O, what a beast was I to chide at him!

Nurse. Will you speak well of him that killed your
105   cousin?

Juliet. Shall I speak ill of him that is my husband?
    Ah, poor my lord, what tongue shall smooth thy
      name
    When I, thy three-hours' wife, have mangled it?
110   But wherefore, villain, didst thou kill my cousin?
    That villain cousin would have killed my husband.
    Back, foolish tears, back to your native spring!
    Your tributary drops belong to woe,
    Which you, mistaking, offer up to joy.
115   My husband lives, that Tybalt would have slain;
    And Tybalt's dead, that would have slain my
      husband.
    All this is comfort; wherefore weep I then?
    Some word there was, worser than Tybalt's death,
120   That murdered me. I would forget it fain;
    But O, it presses to my memory
    Like damned guilty deeds to sinners' minds!
    "Tybalt is dead, and Romeo—banished."
    That "banished," that one word "banished,"
125   Hath slain ten thousand Tybalts. Tybalt's death
    Was woe enough, if it had ended there;
    Or, if sour woe delights in fellowship
    And needly will be ranked with other griefs,
    Why followed not, when she said "Tybalt's dead,"
130   Thy father, or thy mother, nay, or both,
    Which modern lamentation might have moved?
    But with a rearward following Tybalt's death,
    "Romeo is banished"—to speak that word
    Is father, mother, Tybalt, Romeo, Juliet,
135   All slain, all dead. "Romeo is banished"—
    There is no end, no limit, measure, bound,
    In that word's death; no words can that woe sound.

144 **beguiled:** cheated.

147-149 **But I . . . maidenhead:** I will die a widow without ever really having been a wife. Death, not Romeo, will be my husband.

151 **wot:** know.

3-4 **Affliction . . . calamity:** Trouble follows you everywhere.

Where is my father and my mother, nurse?

Nurse. Weeping and wailing over Tybalt's corse.
140   Will you go to them? I will bring you thither.

Juliet. Wash they his wounds with tears? Mine shall be
        spent,
    When theirs are dry, for Romeo's banishment.
    Take up those cords. Poor ropes, you are beguiled,
145   Both you and I, for Romeo is exiled.
    He made you for a highway to my bed;
    But I, a maid, die maiden-widowed.
    Come, cords; come, nurse. I'll to my wedding bed;
    And death, not Romeo, take my maidenhead!

150   **Nurse.** Hie to your chamber. I'll find Romeo
        To comfort you. I wot well where he is.
        Hark ye, your Romeo will be here at night.
        I'll to him; he is hid at Laurence' cell.

    Juliet. O, find him! give this ring to my true knight
155   And bid him come to take his last farewell.

    [Exeunt.]

Scene 3 *Friar Laurence's cell.*

> *Friar Laurence tells Romeo of his banishment,
> and Romeo collapses in grief. When he learns
> from the Nurse that Juliet, too, is in despair, he
> threatens to stab himself. The friar reacts by
> suggesting a plan. Romeo is to spend a few
> hours with Juliet and then escape to Mantua.
> While he is away, the friar will announce the
> wedding and try to get a pardon from the
> Prince.*

[Enter Friar Laurence.]

Friar Laurence. Romeo, come forth; come forth, thou
        fearful man.
    Affliction is enamored of thy parts,

5 doom: sentence.

11 doomsday: death.

12 vanished: came.

15 *Why does Romeo think death would be a more merciful punishment than banishment?*

20-26 without: outside. Being exiled to the rest of the world (that is, the world away from Juliet) is as bad as being dead. And yet you smile at my misfortune!

27-31 The Friar is very angry at Romeo's reaction to the news. He reminds Romeo that the crime he committed deserves the death penalty, according to law. The Prince has shown Romeo mercy, and Romeo doesn't appreciate it.

32-46 Romeo refuses to listen to reason. He is obsessed with the word *banished,* just as Juliet was. He compares himself to the animals—and even the flies that live off the dead *(carrion)*—that will be able to see Juliet while he will not.

And thou art wedded to calamity.

[Enter Romeo.]

5 **Romeo.** Father, what news? What is the Prince's doom?
What sorrow craves acquaintance at my hand
That I yet know not?

Friar Laurence. Too familiar
Is my dear son with such sour company.
10 I bring thee tidings of the Prince's doom.

Romeo. What less than doomsday is the Prince's doom?

Friar Laurence. A gentler judgment vanished from his
lips—
Not body's death, but body's banishment.

15 **Romeo.** Ha, banishment? Be merciful, say "death";
For exile hath more terror in his look,
Much more than death. Do not say "banishment."

Friar Laurence. Hence from Verona art thou banished.
Be patient, for the world is broad and wide.

20 **Romeo.** There is no world without Verona walls,
But purgatory, torture, hell itself.
Hence banished is banisht from the world,
And world's exile is death. Then "banishment,"
Is death mistermed. Calling death "banishment,"
25 Thou cuttst my head off with a golden axe
And smilest upon the stroke that murders me.

Friar Laurence. O deadly sin! O rude unthankfulness!
Thy fault our law calls death; but the kind Prince,
Taking thy part, hath rushed aside the law,
30 And turned that black word death to banishment.
This is dear mercy, and thou seest it not.

Romeo. 'Tis torture, and not mercy. Heaven is here,
Where Juliet lives; and every cat and dog
And little mouse, every unworthy thing,
35 Live here in heaven and may look on her;

47-49 *Hadst . . . to kill me:* Couldn't you have killed me with poison or a knife instead of with that awful word?

55 *fond:* foolish.

60-62 The Friar offers philosophical comfort and counseling *(adversity's sweet milk)* as a way to overcome hardship.

But Romeo may not. More validity,
More honorable state, more courtship lives
In carrion flies than Romeo. They may seize
On the white wonder of dear Juliet's hand
40   And steal immortal blessing from her lips,
Who, even in pure and vestal modesty,
Still blush, as thinking their own kisses sin;
But Romeo may not—he is banished.
This may flies do, when I from this must fly;
45   They are free men, but I am banished.
And sayst thou yet that exile is not death?
Hadst thou no poison mixed, no sharp-ground knife,
No sudden mean of death, though ne'er so mean,
But "banished" to kill me—"banished"?
50   O friar, the damned use that word in hell;
Howling attends it! How hast thou the heart,
Being a divine, a ghostly confessor,
A sin-absolver, and my friend professed,
To mangle me with that word "banished"?

55   **Friar Laurence.** Thou fond mad man, hear me a little
          speak.

Romeo. O, thou wilt speak again of banishment.

Friar Laurence. I'll give thee armor to keep off that
          word;
60   Adversity's sweet milk, philosophy,
To comfort thee, though thou art banished.

Romeo. Yet "banished"? Hang up philosophy!
Unless philosophy can make a Juliet,
Displant a town, reverse a prince's doom,
65   It helps not, it prevails not. Talk no more.

Friar Laurence. O, then I see that madmen have no
          ears.

Romeo. How should they, when that wise men have
          no eyes?

70 *dispute:* discuss; *estate:* situation.

71-79 You can't understand how I feel because you haven't been through what I have.

80-91 When a knock sounds, the Friar frantically tries to get Romeo to hide.

Friar Laurence. Let me dispute with thee of thy estate.

70

Romeo. Thou canst not speak of that thou dost not
feel.
Wert thou as young as I, Juliet thy love,
An hour but married, Tybalt murdered,
Doting like me, and like me banished,
Then mightst thou speak, then mightst thou tear
thy hair,
And fall upon the ground, as I do now,
Taking the measure of an unmade grave.

75

[Nurse knocks within.]

Friar Laurence. Arise; one knocks. Good Romeo, hide
thyself.

80

Romeo. Not I; unless the breath of heartsick groans
Mist-like infold me from the search of eyes.

[Knock.]

Friar Laurence. Hark, how they knock! Who's there?
Romeo, arise;
Thou wilt be taken.—Stay awhile!—Stand up;

85

[Knock.]

Run to my study.—By-and-by!—God's will,
What simpleness is this.—I come, I come!

[Knock.]

Who knocks so hard? Whence come you? What's
your will?

90

Nurse. *[Within.]* Let me come in, and you shall know
my errand.
I come from Lady Juliet.

Friar Laurence.   Welcome then.

[Enter Nurse.]

Nurse. O holy friar, O, tell me, holy friar,

95

99-105 *O, he . . . an O:* The Nurse says that Romeo is in exactly the same condition as Juliet. She tells Romeo to stand up and be a man and asks why he's in such deep grief *(so deep an O).*

113 *concealed lady:* secret bride.

118-124 *that name:* the name *Romeo.* Romeo says his name is a bullet that kills Juliet just as his hand killed her kinsman Tybalt. Romeo asks where in his body *(hateful mansion)* his name can be found so that he can cut the name out. *What is Romeo about to do?*

125-142 *Hold:* stop. You're not acting like a man. Would you send your soul to hell by committing suicide *(doing damned hate)?* Why do you curse your birth, heaven, and earth? You are refusing to make good use of your advantages just as a miser refuses to spend his money.

Where is my lady's lord, where's Romeo?

Friar Laurence. There on the ground, with his own
tears made drunk.

Nurse. O, he is even in my mistress' case,
100   Just in her case! O woeful sympathy!
Piteous predicament! Even so lies she,
Blubb'ring and weeping, weeping and blubbering.
Stand up, stand up! Stand, an you be a man.
For Juliet's sake, for her sake, rise and stand!
105   Why should you fall into so deep an O?

Romeo. *[Rises]* Nurse—

Nurse. Ah sir! ah sir! Well, death's the end of all.

Romeo. Spakest thou of Juliet? How is it with her?
Doth not she think me an old murderer,
110   Now I have stained the childhood of our joy
With blood removed but little from her own?
Where is she? and how doth she? and what says
My concealed lady to our canceled love?

Nurse. O, she says nothing, sir, but weeps and weeps;
115   And now falls on her bed; and then starts up,
And Tybalt calls; and then on Romeo cries,
And then down falls again.

Romeo.   As if that name,
Shot from the deadly level of a gun,
120   Did murder her; as that name's cursed hand
Murdered her kinsman. O tell me, friar, tell me,
In what vile part of this anatomy
Doth my name lodge? Tell me, that I may sack
The hateful mansion.

[Draws his dagger.]

125   **Friar Laurence.**   Hold thy desperate hand.
Art thou a man? Thy form cries out thou art;
Thy tears are womanish, thy wild acts denote
The unreasonable fury of a beast.

152-158 The Friar tells Romeo to count his blessings instead of feeling sorry for himself. He lists the things Romeo has to be thankful for. *What three blessings does the Friar mention?*

163-166 Go and spend the night with Juliet. But leave before the guards take their places at the city gates, so you can escape to Mantua.

– Unseemly woman in a seeming man!
130   Or ill-beseeming beast in seeming both!
Thou hast amazed me. By my holy order,
I thought thy disposition better tempered.
Hast thou slain Tybalt? Wilt thou slay thyself?
And slay thy lady too that lives in thee,
135   By doing damned hate upon thyself?
Why railst thou on thy birth, the heaven, and earth?
Since birth and heaven and earth, all three do meet
In thee at once; which thou at once wouldst lose.
Fie, fie, thou shamest thy shape, thy love, thy wit,
140   Which, like a usurer, aboundst in all,
And usest none in that true use indeed
Which should bedeck thy shape, thy love, thy wit.
Thy noble shape is but a form of wax,
Digressing from the valor of a man;
145   Thy dear love sworn but hollow perjury,
Killing that love which thou hast vowed to cherish;
Thy wit, that ornament to shape and love,
Misshapen in the conduct of them both,
Like powder in a skilless soldier's flask,
150   Is set afire by thine own ignorance,
And thou dismembered with thine own defense.
– What, rouse thee, man! Thy Juliet is alive,
For whose dear sake thou wast but lately dead.
There art thou happy. Tybalt would kill thee,
155   But thou slewest Tybalt. There art thou happy.
The law, that threatened death, becomes thy friend
–And turns it to exile. There art thou happy.
A pack of blessings light upon thy back;
Happiness courts thee in her best array;
160   But, like a misbehaved and sullen wench,
Thou poutst upon thy fortune and thy love.
–Take heed, take heed, for such die miserable.
Go get thee to thy love, as was decreed,
Ascend her chamber, hence and comfort her.
165   But look thou stay not till the watch be set,
For then thou canst not pass to Mantua,

167-171 *till we . . . lamentation:* The Friar intends to
announce *(blaze)* the marriage at the right time, get
the families *(friends)* to stop their feud, ask the Prince
to pardon Romeo, and have Romeo return to a happier
situation.

176-177 *How does the Nurse react to the advice the Friar has
just given Romeo?*

179 *bid . . . chide:* Tell Juliet to get ready to scold me for
the way I've behaved.

182 *How has Romeo's mood changed since he threatened
to kill himself?*

183-189 *and here . . . here:* This is what your fate depends on:
either leave before the night watchmen go on duty, or
get out at dawn in a disguise. Stay awhile in Mantua.
I'll find your servant and send messages to you about
what good things are happening here.

Where thou shalt live till we can find a time
To blaze your marriage, reconcile your friends,
Beg pardon of the Prince, and call thee back

170   With twenty hundred thousand times more joy
Than thou wentst forth in lamentation.
Go before, nurse. Commend me to thy lady,
And bid her hasten all the house to bed,
Which heavy sorrow makes them apt unto.

175   Romeo is coming.

Nurse. O Lord, I could have stayed here all the night
To hear good counsel. O, what learning is!
My lord, I'll tell my lady you will come.

Romeo. Do so, and bid my sweet prepare to chide.

[Nurse offers to go and turns again.]

180   **Nurse.** Here is a ring she bid me give you, sir.
Hie you, make haste, for it grows very late.

[Exit.]

Romeo. How well my comfort is revived by this!

Friar Laurence. Go hence; good night; and here stands
all your state:

185   Either be gone before the watch be set,
Or by the break of day disguised from hence.
Sojourn in Mantua. I'll find out your man,
And he shall signify from time to time
Every good hap to you that chances here.

190   Give me thy hand. 'Tis late. Farewell; good night.

Romeo. But that a joy past joy calls out on me,
It were a grief so brief to part with thee.
Farewell.

[Exeunt.]

1-2 Such terrible things have happened that we haven't had time to persuade *(move)* Juliet to think about your marriage proposal.

8 Sad times are not good times for talking of marriage.

11-13 *and know . . . heaviness:* I'll know early tomorrow what she intends to do; tonight she's locked up with her sorrow. *What reason do Lord and Lady Capulet think causes Juliet to be sad?*

14-31 Capulet thinks Juliet will obey him and pledges her in marriage to Paris (makes a *desperate tender,* or bold offer). He decides the wedding will be on Thursday and only a small ceremony, since the family is mourning Tybalt's death. He is so sure that Juliet will accept Paris that he calls Paris "son" already.

Scene 4 *Capulet's house.*

In this scene, Paris visits the Capulets, who are mourning the death of Tybalt. He says he realizes that this is no time to talk of marriage. Capulet, however, disagrees; he decides that Juliet should marry Paris on Thursday, three days away. He tells Lady Capulet to inform Juliet immediately.

[Enter Capulet, Lady Capulet, and Paris.]

Capulet. Things have fall'n out, sir, so unluckily
That we have had no time to move our daughter.
Look you, she loved her kinsman Tybalt dearly,
And so did I. Well, we were born to die.
5 'Tis very late; she'll not come down tonight.
I promise you, but for your company,
I would have been abed an hour ago.

Paris. These times of woe afford no time to woo.
Madam, good night. Commend me to your
10   daughter.

Lady Capulet. I will, and know her mind early
    tomorrow;
Tonight she's mewed up to her heaviness.

[Paris offers to go and Capulet calls him again.]

Capulet. Sir Paris, I will make a desperate tender
15 Of my child's love. I think she will be ruled
In all respects by me; nay more, I doubt it not.
Wife, go you to her ere you go to bed;
Acquaint her here of my son Paris' love
And bid her (mark you me?) on Wednesday next—
20 But, soft! what day is this?

Paris.   Monday, my lord.

Capulet. Monday! ha, ha! Well, Wednesday is too soon.
A Thursday let it be—a Thursday, tell her,

34-36 Capulet tells his wife to go to Juliet right away and inform her of his decision .

37-38 *it is . . . by-and-by:* It's so late at night that soon we'll be calling it early in the morning.

She shall be married to this noble earl.
25 Will you be ready? Do you like this haste?
We'll keep no great ado—a friend or two;
For hark you, Tybalt being slain so late,
It may be thought we held him carelessly,
Being our kinsman, if we revel much.
30 Therefore we'll have some half a dozen friends,
And there an end. But what say you to Thursday?

Paris. My lord, I would that Thursday were tomorrow.

Capulet. Well, get you gone. A Thursday be it then.
Go you to Juliet ere you go to bed;
35 Prepare her, wife, against this wedding day.
Farewell, my lord.—Light to my chamber, ho!
Afore me, it is so very very late
That we may call it early by-and-by.
Good night.

[Exeunt.]

Scene 5 *Capulet's orchard.*

Romeo and Juliet have spent the night together, but before daylight, Romeo leaves for Mantua. As soon as he leaves, Lady Capulet comes in to tell Juliet of her father's decision—that she will marry Count Paris on Thursday. Juliet is very upset and refuses to go along with the plan. Juliet's father goes into a rage at her disobedience and tells her that she will marry Paris or he will disown her.

The Nurse advises Juliet to wed Paris, since her marriage to Romeo is over and Paris is a better man anyway. Juliet, now angry with the Nurse, decides to go to Friar Laurence for help.

[Enter Romeo and Juliet *above, at the window.*]

2-5 ***It was . . . nightingale:*** The nightingale sings at night; the lark sings in the morning. *What is Juliet trying to get Romeo to believe?*

6 ***herald:*** messenger.

9-10 ***night's candles:*** stars. *How is day personified here?*

12-25 Juliet continues to pretend it is night to keep Romeo from leaving, even though she knows that it is morning. Romeo gives in and says he'll stay if Juliet wishes it, even if staying means death.

26-28 Romeo's mention of death frightens Juliet. She becomes serious and urges Romeo to go quickly.

29 ***division:*** melody.

31-34 The toad's large, brilliant eyes would be more suitable for the lark. ***affray:*** frighten. ***hunt's-up:*** a morning song for hunters.

Juliet. Wilt thou be gone? It is not yet near day.
It was the nightingale, and not the lark,
That pierced the fearful hollow of thine ear.
Nightly she sings on yond pomegranate tree.
5   Believe me, love, it was the nightingale.

Romeo. It was the lark, the herald of the morn;
No nightingale. Look, love, what envious streaks
Do lace the severing clouds in yonder East.
Night's candles are burnt out, and jocund day
10   Stands tiptoe on the misty mountain tops.
I must be gone and live, or stay and die.

Juliet. Yond light is not daylight; I know it, I.
It is some meteor that the sun exhales
To be to thee this night a torchbearer
15   And light thee on thy way to Mantua.
Therefore stay yet; thou needst not to be gone.

Romeo. Let me be ta'en, let me be put to death.
I am content, so thou wilt have it so.
I'll say yon grey is not the morning's eye,
20   'Tis but the pale reflex of Cynthia's brow;
Nor that is not the lark whose notes do beat
The vaulty heaven so high above our heads.
I have more care to stay than will to go.
Come, death, and welcome! Juliet wills it so.
25   How is't, my soul? Let's talk; it is not day.

Juliet. It is, it is! Hie hence, be gone, away!
It is the lark that sings so out of tune,
Straining harsh discords and unpleasing sharps.
Some say the lark makes sweet division;
30   This doth not so, for she divideth us.
Some say the lark and loathed toad changed eyes;
O, now I would they had changed voices too,
Since arm from arm that voice doth us affray,
Hunting thee hence with hunt's-up to the day!
35   O, now be gone! More light and light it grows.

47 *much in years:* very old.

55-57 *I have . . . tomb:* Juliet sees an evil vision of the future. *What is her vision?*

60 *Dry . . . blood:* People believed that sorrow drained the blood from the heart, causing a sad person to look pale. Romeo leaves Juliet by climbing down from her balcony.

Romeo. More light and light—more dark and dark our
woes!

[Enter Nurse, *hastily.*]

Nurse. Madam!

Juliet. Nurse?

40 **Nurse.** Your lady mother is coming to your chamber.
The day is broke; be wary, look about.

[Exit.]

Juliet. Then, window, let day in, and let life out.

Romeo. Farewell, farewell! One kiss, and I'll descend.

[He starts down the ladder.]

Juliet. Art thou gone so, my lord, my love, my friend?
45 I must hear from thee every day in the hour,
For in a minute there are many days.
O, by this count I shall be much in years
Ere I again behold my Romeo!

Romeo. Farewell!
50 I will omit no opportunity
That may convey my greetings, love, to thee.

Juliet. O, thinkst thou we shall ever meet again?

Romeo. I doubt it not; and all these woes shall serve
For sweet discourses in our time to come.

55 **Juliet.** O God, I have an ill-divining soul!
Methinks I see thee, now thou art below,
As one dead in the bottom of a tomb.
Either my eyesight fails, or thou lookst pale.

Romeo. And trust me, love, in my eye so do you.
60 Dry sorrow drinks our blood. Adieu! adieu!

[Exit.]

61-63 *fickle:* changeable in loyalty or affection. Juliet asks fickle Fortune why it has anything to do with Romeo, who is the opposite of fickle.

69 *What . . . hither:* What unusual reason brings her here?

72-74 *What does Lady Capulet think Juliet is crying about?*

76-78 *have . . . wit:* stop crying *(have done).* A little grief is evidence of love, while too much grief shows a lack of good sense *(want of wit).*

Juliet. O Fortune, Fortune! all men call thee fickle.
If thou art fickle, what dost thou with him
That is renowned for faith? Be fickle, Fortune,
For then I hope thou wilt not keep him long
65 But send him back.

Lady Capulet. *[Within.]* Ho, daughter! are you up?

Juliet. Who is't that calls? It is my lady mother.
Is she not down so late, or up so early?
What unaccustomed cause procures her hither?

[Enter Lady Capulet.]

70 **Lady Capulet.** Why, how now, Juliet?

Juliet.   Madam, I am not well.

Lady Capulet. Evermore weeping for your cousin's
death?
What, wilt thou wash him from his grave with tears?
75 An if thou couldst, thou couldst not make him live.
Therefore have done. Some grief shows much of
love;
But much of grief shows still some want of wit.

Juliet. Yet let me weep for such a feeling loss.

80 **Lady Capulet.** So shall you feel the loss, but not the
friend
Which you weep for.

Juliet.   Feeling so the loss,
I cannot choose but ever weep the friend.

85 **Lady Capulet.** Well, girl, thou weepst not so much for
his death
As that the villain lives which slaughtered him.

Juliet. What villain, madam?

Lady Capulet.   That same villain Romeo.

90-114 In these lines Juliet's words have double meanings. In order to avoid lying to her mother, she chooses her words carefully. They can mean what her mother wants to hear, but they can also mean what we know Juliet really has in mind.

101 *runagate:* runaway.

102 *unaccustomed dram:* poison. *What does Lady Capulet plan to do about Romeo?*

105-114 *Dead* could refer either to Romeo or to Juliet's heart. Juliet says that if her mother could find someone to carry a poison to Romeo, she would mix *(temper)* it herself. *What hidden meaning lies In lines 108-112?*

Juliet. *[Aside.]* Villain and he be many miles
    asunder.—
    God pardon him! I do, with all my heart;
    And yet no man like he doth grieve my heart.

Lady Capulet. That is because the traitor murderer
    lives.

Juliet. Ay, madam, from the reach of these my hands.
    Would none but I might venge my cousin's death!

Lady Capulet. We will have vengeance for it, fear
    thou not.
    Then weep no more. I'll send to one in Mantua,
    Where that same banished runagate doth live,
    Shall give him such an unaccustomed dram
    That he shall soon keep Tybalt company;
    And then I hope thou wilt be satisfied.

Juliet. Indeed I never shall be satisfied
    With Romeo till I behold him—dead—
    Is my poor heart so for a kinsman vexed.
    Madam, if you could find out but a man
    To bear a poison, I would temper it;
    That Romeo should, upon receipt thereof,
    Soon sleep in quiet. O, how my heart abhors
    To hear him named and cannot come to him,
    To wreak the love I bore my cousin Tybalt
    Upon his body that hath slaughtered him!

Lady Capulet. Find thou the means, and I'll find such
    a man.
    But now I'll tell thee joyful tidings, girl.

Juliet. And joy comes well in such a needy time.
    What are they, I beseech your ladyship?

Lady Capulet. Well, well, thou hast a careful father,
    child;
    One who, to put thee from thy heaviness,
    Hath sorted out a sudden day of joy

136-138 ***and when . . . Paris:*** Once again, Juliet uses a double meaning. She mentions Romeo to show her mother how strongly opposed she is to marrying Paris, yet what she really means is that she loves Romeo.

143 ***my brother's son:*** Tybalt.

145-153 ***conduit:*** fountain. Capulet compares Juliet to a boat, an ocean, and the wind because of her excessive crying.

That thou expects not nor I looked not for.

125 **Juliet.** Madam, in happy time! What day is that?

Lady Capulet. Marry, my child, early next Thursday
    morn
The gallant, young, and noble gentleman,
The County Paris, at Saint Peter's Church,
130 Shall happily make thee there a joyful bride.

Juliet. Now by Saint Peter's Church, and Peter too,
He shall not make me there a joyful bride!
I wonder at this haste, that I must wed
Ere he that should be husband comes to woo.
135 I pray you tell my lord and father, madam,
I will not marry yet; and when I do, I swear
It shall be Romeo, whom you know I hate,
Rather than Paris. These are news indeed!

Lady Capulet. Here comes your father. Tell him so
140   yourself,
And see how he will take it at your hands.

[Enter Capulet and Nurse.]

Capulet. When the sun sets the air doth drizzle dew,
But for the sunset of my brother's son
It rains downright.
145 How now? a conduit, girl? What, still in tears?
Evermore show'ring? In one little body
Thou counterfeitst a bark, a sea, a wind:
For still thy eyes, which I may call the sea,
Do ebb and flow with tears; the bark thy body is,
150 Sailing in this salt flood; the winds, thy sighs,
Who, raging with thy tears and they with them,
Without a sudden calm will overset
Thy tempest-tossed body. How now, wife?
Have you delivered to her our decree?

155 **Lady Capulet.** Ay, sir; but she will none, she gives you
    thanks.

158 ***take me with you:*** Let me understand you. Capulet, like his wife, simply can't believe that Juliet won't go along with his plan for marriage.

164-166 I'm not pleased, but I am grateful for your intentions.

167-176 ***How . . . tallow-face:*** Capulet is furious with Juliet. He rages, calls her names, and threatens her. He calls her a person who argues over fine points ***(choplogic),*** and says she is a spoiled child ***(minion).*** He tells her to prepare herself ***(fettle your fine joints)*** for the wedding or he'll haul her there in a cart for criminals ***(hurdle).*** He calls her an anemic piece of dead flesh ***(green-sickness carrion)*** and a coward ***(tallow-face).***

177 ***Fie . . . mad:*** Lady Capulet is worried by her husband's violent anger and tries to calm him.

185 ***My fingers itch:*** I feel like hitting you.

189 ***hilding:*** good-for-nothing person.

I would the fool were married to her grave!

Capulet. Soft! take me with you, take me with you,
    wife.
160   How? Will she none? Doth she not give us thanks?
    Is she not proud? Doth she not count her blest,
    Unworthy as she is, that we have wrought
    So worthy a gentleman to be her bridegroom?

Juliet. Not proud you have, but thankful that you have.
165   Proud can I never be of what I hate,
    But thankful even for hate that is meant love.

Capulet. How, how, how, how, choplogic? What is this?
    "Proud"—and "I thank you"—and "I thank you
    not"—
170   And yet "not proud"? Mistress minion you,
    Thank me no thankings, nor proud me no prouds,
    But fettle your fine joints 'gainst Thursday next
    To go with Paris to Saint Peter's Church,
    Or I will drag thee on a hurdle thither.
175   Out, you green-sickness carrion! out, you baggage!
    You tallow-face!

Lady Capulet.   Fie, fie; what, are you mad?

Juliet. Good father, I beseech you on my knees,

[She kneels down.]

Hear me with patience but to speak a word.

180 **Capulet.** Hang thee, young baggage! disobedient
    wretch!
    I tell thee what—get thee to church a Thursday
    Or never after look me in the face.
    Speak not, reply not, do not answer me!
185   My fingers itch. Wife, we scarce thought us blest
    That God had lent us but this only child;
    But now I see this one is one too much,
    And that we have a curse in having her.
    Out on her, hilding!

190-197   The Nurse dares to stand up for Juliet but is rudely
dismissed by Capulet, who considers her nothing more
than a lowly servant.

194   *Smatter:* chatter.

199   *Utter . . . bowl:* Save your words of wisdom for a
gathering of gossips.

202-223   Capulet complains that day and night he's tried to get
Juliet a good husband, and now that he has, she acts
like a crying *(puling)* fool, a whining doll *(mammet).*
He will not put up with this. She will marry or he'll put
her out of his house. He will not break his promise to
Paris *(be forsworn).*

190 **Nurse.**   God in heaven bless her!
    You are to blame, my lord, to rate her so.

Capulet. And why, my Lady Wisdom? Hold your
    tongue,
    Good Prudence. Smatter with your gossips, go!

195 **Nurse.** I speak no treason.

Capulet.   O, God-i-god-en!

Nurse. May not one speak?

Capulet.   Peace, you mumbling fool!
    Utter your gravity o'er a gossip's bowl,
200   For here we need it not.

Lady Capulet.   You are too hot.

Capulet. God's bread! it makes me mad. Day, night,
    late, early,
    At home, abroad, alone, in company,
205   Waking or sleeping, still my care hath been
    To have her matched; and having now provided
    A gentleman of princely parentage,
    Of fair demesnes, youthful, and nobly trained,
    Stuffed, as they say, with honorable parts,
210   Proportioned as one's thought would wish a man—
    And then to have a wretched puling fool,
    A whining mammet, in her fortunes tender,
    To answer "I'll not wed, I cannot love;
    I am too young, I pray you pardon me"!
215   But, an you will not wed, I'll pardon you.
    Graze where you will, you shall not house with me.
    Look to't, think on't; I do not use to jest.
    Thursday is near; lay hand on heart, advise:
    An you be mine, I'll give you to my friend;
220   An you be not, hang, beg, starve, die in the streets,
    For, by my soul, I'll ne'er acknowledge thee,
    Nor what is mine shall never do thee good.
    Trust to't. Bethink you. I'll not be forsworn.

[Exit.]

233-237 ***How shall . . . earth:*** Juliet is worried about the sin of being married to two men. She goes on to ask how heaven can play such tricks ***(practice stratagems)*** on her.

242-251 The Nurse gives Juliet advice. She says that since Romeo is banished, he's no good to her; Juliet should marry Paris. Romeo is a dishcloth ***(dishclout)*** compared to Paris.

251 ***beshrew:*** curse.

252-254 This new marriage will be better than the first, which is as good as over.

Juliet. Is there no pity sitting in the clouds
225   That sees into the bottom of my grief?
     O sweet my mother, cast me not away!
     Delay this marriage for a month, a week;
     Or if you do not, make the bridal bed
     In that dim monument where Tybalt lies.

230   **Lady Capulet.** Talk not to me, for I'll not speak a
        word.
     Do as thou wilt, for I have done with thee.

[Exit.]

Juliet. O God!—O nurse, how shall this be prevented?
     My husband is on earth, my faith in heaven.
235   How shall that faith return again to earth
     Unless that husband send it me from heaven
     By leaving earth? Comfort me, counsel me.
     Alack, alack, that heaven should practice stratagems
     Upon so soft a subject as myself!
240   What sayst thou? Hast thou not a word of joy?
     Some comfort, nurse.

Nurse.   Faith, here it is.
     Romeo is banisht; and all the world to nothing
     That he dares ne'er come back to challenge you;
245   Or if he do, it needs must be by stealth.
     Then, since the case so stands as now it doth,
     I think it best you married with the County.
     O, he's a lovely gentleman!
     Romeo's a dishclout to him. An eagle, madam,
250   Hath not so green, so quick, so fair an eye
     As Paris hath. Beshrew my very heart,
     I think you are happy in this second match,
     For it excels your first; or if it did not,
     Your first is dead—or 'twere as good he were
255   As living here and you no use of him.

Juliet. Speakst thou this from thy heart?

Nurse. And from my soul too; else beshrew them both.

258 *Amen:* I agree. Curse your heart and soul!

260-269 *What message does Juliet give to the Nurse for her parents?*

265-270 Now that Juliet is alone, she says what she really thinks. She calls the Nurse an old devil *(ancient damnation).* She doesn't know whether to be angrier at the Nurse for telling her to break her wedding vows or for criticizing Romeo after having praised him. *Go . . . twain:* Leave me. You and my secrets will be separated *(twain)* from now on. *How has Juliet's relationship with the Nurse changed?*

Juliet. Amen!

Nurse. What?

260 **Juliet.** Well, thou hast comforted me marvelous much.
      Go in; and tell my lady I am gone,
      Having displeased my father, to Laurence' cell,
      To make confession and to be absolved.

Nurse. Marry, I will; and this is wisely done.

[Exit.]

265 **Juliet.** Ancient damnation! O most wicked fiend!
      Is it more sin to wish me thus forsworn,
      Or to dispraise my lord with that same tongue
      Which she hath praised him with above compare
      So many thousand times? Go, counselor!
270   Thou and my bosom henceforth shall be twain.
      I'll to the friar to know his remedy.
      If all else fail, myself have power to die.

[Exit.]

3-4 **My . . . haste:** Capulet is eager to have the wedding on Thursday and so am I.

5-7 **You say . . . not:** You don't know how Juliet feels about this. It's a difficult *(uneven)* plan, and I don't like it. *What is the Friar's real reason for wanting to slow down the wedding preparations?*

8-17 *According to Paris, what is Capulet's reason for wanting Juliet to marry so quickly?*

ACT FOUR

Act 4, scene 1

Scene 1 *Friar Laurence's cell.*

When Juliet arrives at Friar Laurence's cell she is upset to find Paris there making arrangements for their wedding. When Paris leaves, the panicked Juliet tells the Friar that if he has no solution to her problem, she will kill herself. The Friar explains his plan. Juliet will drink a potion he has made from his herbs that will put her in a deathlike coma. When she wakes up two days later in the family tomb, Romeo will be waiting for her, and they will escape to Mantua together.

[Enter Friar Laurence and Paris.]

Friar Laurence. On Thursday, sir? The time is very
    short.

Paris. My father Capulet will have it so,
    And I am nothing slow to slack his haste.

5 **Friar Laurence.** You say you do not know the lady's
    mind.
    Uneven is the course; I like it not.

Paris. Immoderately she weeps for Tybalt's death,
    And therefore have I little talked of love;
10   For Venus smiles not in a house of tears.
    Now, sir, her father counts it dangerous
    That she do give her sorrow so much sway,
    And in his wisdom hastes our marriage
    To stop the inundation of her tears,
15   Which, too much minded by herself alone,
    May be put from her by society.
    Now do you know the reason of this haste.

22-32 As in the last scene of Act Three, Juliet chooses her words carefully to avoid lying and to avoid telling her secret. *Whom does* him *refer to in line 29?*

34-35 *The tears . . . spite:* The tears haven't ruined my face: it wasn't all that beautiful before they did their damage.

40 Paris says he owns Juliet's face (since she will soon marry him). Insulting her face, he says, insults him, its owner.

Friar Laurence. *[Aside.]* I would I knew not why it
should be slowed.—

20   Look, sir, here comes the lady toward my cell.

[Enter Juliet.*]*

Paris. Happily met, my lady and my wife!

Juliet. That may be, sir, when I may be a wife.

Paris. That may be must be, love, on Thursday next.

Juliet. What must be shall be.

25 **Friar Laurence.**   That's a certain text.

Paris. Come you to make confession to this father?

Juliet. To answer that, I should confess to you.

Paris. Do not deny to him that you love me.

Juliet. I will confess to you that I love him.

30 **Paris.** So will ye, I am sure, that you love me.

Juliet. If I do so, it will be of more price,
Being spoke behind your back, than to your face.

Paris. Poor soul, thy face is much abused with tears.

Juliet. The tears have got small victory by that,
35   For it was bad enough before their spite.

Paris. Thou wrongst it more than tears with that
report.

Juliet. That is no slander, sir, which is a truth;
And what I spake, I spake it to my face.

40 **Paris.** Thy face is mine, and thou hast slandered it.

Juliet. It may be so, for it is not mine own.
Are you at leisure, holy father, now,
Or shall I come to you at evening mass?

Friar Laurence. My leisure serves me, pensive
45   daughter, now.

46 We must ask you to leave.

54-55 *compass:* limit. ***prorogue:*** postpone.

59-62 ***If . . . hands:*** If you can't help me, at least tell me that my plan ***(resolution)*** is right.

64-74 Before I sign another wedding agreement ***(deed),*** I will use this knife to kill myself. If you, with your years of experience ***(long-experienced time),*** can't help me, I'll end my sufferings ***(extremes)*** and solve the problem myself.

79-84 If you are desperate enough to kill yourself, then you'll try the desperate solution I have in mind.

My lord, we must entreat the time alone.

Paris. God shield I should disturb devotion!
Juliet, on Thursday early will I rouse ye.
Till then, adieu, and keep this holy kiss.

[Exit.]

50 **Juliet.** O, shut the door! and when thou hast done so,
Come weep with me—past hope, past cure, past
help!

Friar Laurence. Ah, Juliet, I already know thy grief;
It strains me past the compass of my wits.
55 I hear thou must, and nothing may prorogue it,
On Thursday next be married to this County.

Juliet. Tell me not, friar, that thou hearst of this,
Unless thou tell me how I may prevent it.
If in thy wisdom thou canst give no help,
60 Do thou but call my resolution wise
And with this knife I'll help it presently.
God joined my heart and Romeo's, thou our hands;
And ere this hand, by thee to Romeo's sealed,
Shall be the label to another deed,
65 Or my true heart with treacherous revolt
Turn to another, this shall slay them both.
Therefore, out of thy long-experienced time,
Give me some present counsel; or, behold,
'Twixt my extremes and me this bloody knife
70 Shall play the umpire, arbitrating that
Which the commission of thy years and art
Could to no issue of true honor bring.
Be not so long to speak. I long to die
If what thou speakst not of remedy.

75 **Friar Laurence.** Hold, daughter, I do spy a kind
of hope,
Which craves as desperate an execution
As that is desperate which we would prevent.
If, rather than to marry County Paris,

85-97 Juliet replies that she will do anything. *What does Juliet say she would rather face than marry Paris?* **charnel house:** a storehouse for bones from old graves; **reeky shanks:** stinking bones; **chapless:** without jaws. The description in lines 89-93 comes closer to Juliet's future than she knows.

98-130 The Friar explains his desperate plan to Juliet.

103 *vial:* small bottle.

106 *humor:* liquid.

107-116 Your pulse will stop **(surcease),** and you will turn cold, pale, and stiff, as if you were dead. This condition will last for forty-two hours.

80 Thou hast the strength of will to slay thyself,
    Then is it likely thou wilt undertake
    A thing like death to chide away this shame,
    That copest with death himself to scape from it;
    And, if thou darest, I'll give thee remedy.

85 **Juliet.** O, bid me leap, rather than marry Paris,
    From off the battlements of yonder tower,
    Or walk in thievish ways, or bid me lurk
    Where serpents are; chain me with roaring bears,
    Or shut me nightly in a charnel house,
90 O'ercovered quite with dead men's rattling bones,
    With reeky shanks and yellow chapless skulls;
    Or bid me go into a new-made grave
    And hide me with a dead man in his shroud—
    Things that, to hear them told, have made me
95   tremble—
    And I will do it without fear or doubt,
    To live an unstained wife to my sweet love.

    Friar Laurence. Hold, then. Go home, be merry, give
        consent
100 To marry Paris. Wednesday is tomorrow.
    Tomorrow night look that thou lie alone:
    Let not the nurse lie with thee in thy chamber.
    Take thou this vial, being then in bed,
    And this distilled liquor drink thou off;
105 When presently through all thy veins shall run
    A cold and drowsy humor; for no pulse
    Shall keep his native progress, but surcease;
    No warmth, no breath, shall testify thou livest;
    The roses in thy lips and cheeks shall fade
110 To paly ashes, thy eyes' windows fall
    Like death when he shuts up the day of life;
    Each part, deprived of supple government,
    Shall, stiff and stark and cold, appear like death;
    And in this borrowed likeness of shrunk death
115 Thou shalt continue two-and-forty hours,
    And then awake as from a pleasant sleep.

117-122 *What will happen when Paris comes to wake Juliet on Thursday?*

124 *drift:* plan.

129-130 *inconstant toy:* foolish whim.
Abate thy valor: weaken your courage.

1-8 Capulet is having a cheerful conversation with his servants about the wedding preparations. One servant assures him that he will test *(try)* each cook he hires by making the cook taste his own food *(lick his own fingers).*

Now, when the bridegroom in the morning comes
To rouse thee from thy bed, there art thou dead.
Then, as the manner of our country is,
120 In thy best robes uncovered on the bier
Thou shalt be borne to that same ancient vault
Where all the kindred of the Capulets lie.
In the meantime, against thou shalt awake,
Shall Romeo by my letters know our drift;
125 And hither shall he come; and he and I
Will watch thy waking, and that very night
Shall Romeo bear thee hence to Mantua.
And this shall free thee from this present shame,
If no inconstant toy nor womanish fear
130 Abate thy valor in the acting it.

Juliet. Give me, give me! O, tell me not of fear!

Friar Laurence. Hold! Get you gone, be strong and prosperous
In this resolve. I'll send a friar with speed
135 To Mantua, with my letters to thy lord.

Juliet. Love give me strength! and strength shall help afford.
Farewell, dear father.

[Exeunt.]

Scene 2 *Capulet's house.*

Capulet is making plans for the wedding on Thursday. Juliet arrives and apologizes to him, saying that she will marry Paris. Capulet is so relieved that he reschedules the wedding for the next day, Wednesday.

[Enter Capulet, Lady Capulet, Nurse, *and* Servingmen.]

Capulet. So many guests invite as here are writ.

[Exit a Servingman.]

10 unfurnished: unprepared.

14 A silly, stubborn girl she is. *What does calling Juliet "it" suggest about Capulet's attitude toward her?*

15 shrift: confession.

17-18 How are you, my stubborn *(headstrong)* daughter? ·Where have you been wandering around *(gadding)?*

19-23 Where I . . . pardon: where I have learned to regret disobeying your orders *(behests).* Friar Laurence has ordered *(enjoined)* me to bow before you and ask you to forgive me.

25-26 knot knit up: wedding, from the expression "tying the knot." Capulet declares that the wedding will be the next day, Wednesday, instead of Thursday. *What does moving the wedding up by one day do to Friar Laurence's plan?*

Sirrah, go hire me twenty cunning cooks.

Servingman. You shall have none ill, sir; for I'll try if they can lick their fingers.

5 **Capulet.** How canst thou try them so?

Servingman. Marry, sir, 'tis an ill cook that cannot lick his own fingers. Therefore he that cannot lick his fingers goes not with me.

Capulet. Go, begone.

[*Exit* Servingman.]

10 We shall be much unfurnished for this time.
What, is my daughter gone to Friar Laurence?

Nurse. Ay, forsooth.

Capulet. Well, he may chance to do some good on her.
A peevish self-willed harlotry it is.

[*Enter* Juliet.]

15 **Nurse.** See where she comes from shrift with merry look.

Capulet. How now, my headstrong? Where have you been gadding?

Juliet. Where I have learnt me to repent the sin
20 Of disobedient opposition
To you and your behests, and am enjoined
By holy Laurence to fall prostrate here
To beg your pardon. Pardon, I beseech you!
Henceforward I am ever ruled by you.

25 **Capulet.** Send for the County. Go tell him of this.
I'll have this knot knit up tomorrow morning.

Juliet. I met the youthful lord at Laurence' cell
And gave him what becomed love I might,
Not stepping o'er the bounds of modesty.

30 **Capulet.** Why, I am glad on't. This is well. Stand up.

33-34 *What is ironic about Capulet's praise of Friar Laurence?*

35 *closet:* bedroom.

38-44 Lady Capulet urges her husband to wait until Thursday as originally planned. She needs time to get food *(provision)* ready for the wedding party.

45-51 Capulet is so set on Wednesday that he promises to make the arrangements himself.

This is as't should be. Let me see the County.
Ay, marry, go, I say, and fetch him hither.
Now, afore God, this reverend holy friar,
All our whole city is much bound to him.

35 **Juliet.** Nurse, will you go with me into my closet
To help me sort such needful ornaments
As you think fit to furnish me tomorrow?

Lady Capulet. No, not till Thursday. There is time
enough.

40 **Capulet.** Go, nurse, go with her. We'll to church
tomorrow.

[Exeunt Juliet and Nurse.]

Lady Capulet. We shall be short in our provision.
'Tis now near night.

Capulet. Tush, I will stir about,
45 And all things shall be well, I warrant thee, wife.
Go thou to Juliet, help to deck up her.
I'll not to bed tonight; let me alone.
I'll play the housewife for this once. What, ho!
They are all forth; well, I will walk myself
50 To County Paris, to prepare him up
Against tomorrow. My heart is wondrous light,
Since this same wayward girl is so reclaimed.

[Exeunt.]

Scene 3 *Juliet's bedroom.*

*Juliet sends her mother away and prepares to
take the drug the Friar has given her. She is
confused and frightened but finally puts the
vial to her lips and drinks.*

[Enter Juliet and Nurse.]

Juliet. Ay, those attires are best; but, gentle nurse,

The Tragedy of Romeo and Juliet 187

3-5 *orisons:* prayers. *Why is Juliet's upcoming marriage "cross and full of sin"?*

8-9 *we have . . . tomorrow:* We have picked out *(culled)* everything appropriate for tomorrow.

16-25 *farewell . . . there:* Juliet wonders when she'll see her mother and nurse again. She starts to call back the Nurse but realizes she must be alone to drink the potion. She keeps her knife near her in case the potion doesn't work.

26-31 *Why does Juliet think the Friar might have given her poison?*

32-37 *In these lines what fear does Juliet express?*

I pray thee leave me to myself tonight;
For I have need of many orisons
To move the heavens to smile upon my state,
5   Which, well thou knowest, is cross and full of sin.

[Enter Lady Capulet.]

Lady Capulet. What, are you busy, ho? Need you my
   help?

Juliet. No madam; we have culled such necessaries
   As are behooveful for our state tomorrow.
10   So please you, let me now be left alone,
   And let the nurse this night sit up with you;
   For I am sure you have your hands full all
   In this so sudden business.

Lady Capulet.   Good night.
15   Get thee to bed and rest, for thou hast need.

[Exeunt Lady Capulet and Nurse.]

Juliet. Farewell! God knows when we shall meet again.
   I have a faint cold fear thrills through my veins
   That almost freezes up the heat of life.
   I'll call them back again to comfort me.
20   Nurse!—What should she do here?
   My dismal scene I needs must act alone.
   Come, vial.
   What if this mixture do not work at all?
   Shall I be married then tomorrow morning?
25   No, no! This shall forbid it. Lie thou there.

[Lays down a dagger.]

   What if it be a poison which the friar
   Subtly hath ministered to have me dead,
   Lest in this marriage he should be dishonored
   Because he married me before to Romeo?
30   I fear it is; and yet methinks it should not,
   For he hath still been tried a holy man.
   How if, when I am laid into the tomb,

38-45 Next Juliet fears the vision *(conceit)* she might have on waking in the family tomb and seeing the rotting body of Tybalt.

46-56 She fears that the smells together with sounds of ghosts screaming might make her lose her mind. ***Mandrake*** root was thought to look like the human form and, when pulled from the ground, to scream and drive people mad.

57-60 Juliet thinks she sees Tybalt's ghost searching for Romeo. She cries to the ghost to stop *(stay)* and, with Romeo's name on her lips, quickly drinks the potion.

I wake before the time that Romeo
Come to redeem me? There's a fearful point!
35 Shall I not then be stifled in the vault,
To whose foul mouth no healthsome air breathes in,
And there die strangled ere my Romeo comes?
Or, if I live, is it not very like
The horrible conceit of death and night,
40 Together with the terror of the place—
As in a vault, an ancient receptacle
Where for this many hundred years the bones
Of all my buried ancestors are packed;
Where bloody Tybalt, yet but green in earth,
45 Lies fest'ring in his shroud; where, as they say,
At some hours in the night spirits resort—
Alack, alack, is it not like that I,
So early waking—what with loathsome smells,
And shrieks like mandrakes torn out of the earth,
50 That living mortals, hearing them, run mad—
O, if I wake, shall I not be distraught,
Environed with all these hideous fears,
And madly play with my forefather's joints,
And pluck the mangled Tybalt from his shroud,
55 And, in this rage, with some great kinsman's bone
As with a club dash out my desp'rate brains?
O, look! methinks I see my cousin's ghost
Seeking out Romeo, that did spit his body
Upon a rapier's point. Stay, Tybalt, stay!
60 Romeo, I come! this do I drink to thee.

[She drinks and falls upon her bed within the curtains.]

Scene 4 *Capulet's house.*

*It is now the next morning, nearly time for the
wedding. The household is happy and excited
as everyone makes final preparations.*

[*Enter* Lady Capulet *and* Nurse.]

3 *pastry:* the room where baking is done .

4-6 Capulet tells everyone to wake up *(stir).*

7-8 In his happy mood he even calls the Nurse by her name, Angelica. He tells her to attend to the meat and to spend any amount of money necessary.

9 *cot-quean:* The Nurse playfully calls Capulet a "cottage queen," or a housewife. This is a joke about his doing women's work (arranging the party).

12-13 I've stayed up all night for less important things and never gotten sick.

14-17 Lady and Lord Capulet joke about his being a woman chaser *(mouse-hunt)* as a young man. He jokes about her jealousy *(jealous hood).*

Lady Capulet. Hold, take these keys and fetch more
    spices, nurse.

Nurse. They call for dates and quinces in the pastry.

[Enter Capulet.]

Capulet. Come, stir, stir, stir! The second cock hath
5   crowed,
    The curfew bell hath rung, 'tis three o'clock.
    Look to the baked meat, good Angelica;
    Spare not for cost.

Nurse.   Go, you cot-quean, go,
10   Get you to bed! Faith, you'll be sick tomorrow
    For this night's watching.

Capulet. No, not a whit. What, I have watched ere now
    All night for lesser cause, and ne'er been sick.

Lady Capulet. Ay, you have been a mouse-hunt in your
15   time;
    But I will watch you from such watching now.

[Exeunt Lady Capulet and Nurse.]

Capulet. A jealous hood, a jealous hood!

*[Enter three or four Servants, with spits and logs and
baskets.]*
                       Now, fellow,
    What is there?

20 **First Servant.** Things for the cook, sir; but I know not
    what.

Capulet. Make haste, make haste. *[Exit Servant.]* Sirrah,
    fetch drier logs.
    Call Peter; he will show thee where they are.

25 **Second Servant.** I have a head, sir, that will find out
    logs
    And never trouble Peter for the matter.

28-31 The joking between Capulet and his servants includes the mild oath **Mass,** short for "by the Mass," and **loggerhead,** a word for a stupid person and a pun, since the servant is searching for drier logs. **straight:** right away.

1-12 The Nurse chatters as she bustles around the room arranging things. She calls Juliet a **slugabed,** or sleepyhead, who is trying to get her rest now, since after the wedding, Paris won't let her get much sleep. When Juliet doesn't answer, the Nurse opens the curtains that enclose the bed.

Capulet. Mass, and well said, merry whoreson, ha!
   Thou shalt be loggerhead. *[Exit Servant.]* Good faith,
30   'tis day.
   The County will be here with music straight,
   For so he said he would. *[Music within.]* I hear him
      near.
   Nurse! Wife! What, ho! What, nurse, I say!

[Reenter Nurse.]

35   Go waken Juliet; go and trim her up.
   I'll go and chat with Paris. Hie, make haste,
   Make haste! The bridegroom he is come already:
   Make haste, I say.

[Exeunt.]

Scene 5 *Juliet's bedroom.*

The joyous preparations suddenly change into plans for a funeral when the Nurse discovers Juliet on her bed, apparently dead. Lord and Lady Capulet, Paris, and the Nurse are overcome with grief. Friar Laurence tries to comfort them and instructs them to bring Juliet's body to the Capulet family tomb. The scene abruptly switches to humor, in a foolish conversation between the servant Peter and the musicians hired to play at the wedding.

[Enter Nurse.]

Nurse. Mistress! what, mistress! Juliet! Fast, I warrant
      her, she.
   Why, lamb! why, lady! Fie, you slugabed!
   Why, love, I say! madam! sweetheart! Why, bride!
5   What, not a word? You take your pennyworths now,
   Sleep for a week; for the next night, I warrant,
   The County Paris hath set up his rest
   That you shall rest but little. God forgive me,
   Marry and amen, how sound is she asleep!

The Tragedy of Romeo and Juliet   **195**

17 *aqua vitae:* an alcoholic drink.

19 *lamentable:* filled with grief; mournful.

33-34 *Death . . . field:* What simile does Capulet use to describe what has happened to Juliet?

10　I needs must wake her. Madam, madam, madam!
Aye, let the County take you in your bed,
He'll fright you up, i' faith. Will it not be?

[Opens the curtains.]

What, dressed and in your clothes and down again?
I must needs wake you. Lady! lady! lady!
15　Alas, alas! Help, help! my lady's dead!
O well-a-day that ever I was born!
Some aqua vitae, ho! My lord! my lady!

[Enter Lady Capulet.]

Lady Capulet. What noise is here?

Nurse.　　　　　　　　　　O lamentable day!

20　**Lady Capulet.** What is the matter?

Nurse.　　　　　　　　　Look, look! O heavy day!

Lady Capulet. O me, O me! My child, my only life!
Revive, look up, or I will die with thee!
Help! help! Call help.

[Enter Capulet.]

25　**Capulet.** For shame, bring Juliet forth; her lord is
　　come.

Nurse. She's dead, deceased; she's dead! Alack the day!

Lady Capulet. Alack the day, she's dead, she's dead,
　　she's dead!

30　**Capulet.** Ha! let me see her. Out alas! she's cold,
Her blood is settled, and her joints are stiff;
Life and these lips have long been separated.
Death lies on her like an untimely frost
Upon the sweetest flower of all the field.

35　**Nurse.** O lamentable day!

Lady Capulet.　　　　　　O woeful time!

48 Life . . . Death's: Life, the living, and everything else belongs to Death.

53-57 This is the most miserable hour that time ever saw in its long journey. I had only one child to make me happy, and Death has taken *(catched)* her from me.

64 Beguiled: tricked.

69-70 why . . . solemnity: Why did Death have to come to murder our celebration?

Capulet. Death, that hath ta'en her hence to make me
    wail,
    Ties up my tongue and will not let me speak.

[Enter Friar Laurence *and* Paris, *with* Musicians.*]*

40 **Friar Laurence.** Come, is the bride ready to go to
    church?

Capulet. Ready to go, but never to return.
    O son, the night before thy wedding day
    Hath death lain with thy wife. See, there she lies,
45   Flower as she was, deflowered by him.
    Death is my son-in-law, Death is my heir;
    My daughter he hath wedded. I will die
    And leave him all. Life, living, all is Death's.

Paris. Have I thought long to see this morning's face,
50   And doth it give me such a sight as this?

Lady Capulet. Accursed, unhappy, wretched, hateful
    day!
    Most miserable hour that e'er time saw
    In lasting labor of his pilgrimage!
55   But one, poor one, one poor and loving child,
    But one thing to rejoice and solace in,
    And cruel Death hath catched it from my sight!

Nurse. O woe! O woeful, woeful, woeful day!
    Most lamentable day, most woeful day
60   That ever, ever I did yet behold!
    O day! O day! O day! O hateful day!
    Never was seen so black a day as this.
    O woeful day! O woeful day!

Paris. Beguiled, divorced, wronged, spited, slain!
65   Most detestable Death, by thee beguiled,
    By cruel, cruel thee quite overthrown!
    O love! O life! not life, but love in death!

Capulet. Despised, distressed, hated, martyred, killed!
    Uncomfortable time, why camest thou now

74-88   The Friar comforts the family. He says that the cure for
disaster *(confusion)* cannot be found in cries of grief.
Juliet's family and heaven once shared her; now
heaven has all of her. All the family ever wanted was
the best for her; now she's in heaven—what could be
better than that? It is best to die young, when the soul
is still pure, without sin.

89-93   Do what is customary. Put rosemary, an herb, on her
corpse *(corse)*, and take her, in her finest clothes *(best
array)*, to church. Though it's natural to cry, common
sense tells us we should rejoice for the dead.

94   *ordained festival:* intended for the wedding.

98   *sullen dirges:* sad, mournful tunes.

105-106   *The heavens . . . will:* The fates *(heavens)* frown on
you for some wrong you have done. Don't tempt them
by refusing to accept their will (Juliet's death).

70   To murder, murder our solemnity?
O child! O child! my soul, and not my child!
Dead art thou, dead! alack, my child is dead,
And with my child my joys are buried!

Friar Laurence. Peace, ho, for shame! Confusion's cure
75   lives not
In these confusions. Heaven and yourself
Had part in this fair maid! now heaven hath all,
And all the better is it for the maid.
Your part in her you could not keep from death,
80   But heaven keeps his part in eternal life.
The most you sought was her promotion,
For 'twas your heaven she should be advanced;
And weep ye now, seeing she is advanced
Above the clouds, as high as heaven itself?
85   O, in this love, you love your child so ill
That you run mad, seeing that she is well.
She's not well married that lives married long,
But she's best married that dies married young.
Dry up your tears and stick your rosemary
90   On this fair corse, and, as the custom is,
In all her best array bear her to church;
For though fond nature bids us all lament,
Yet nature's tears are reason's merriment.

Capulet. All things that we ordained festival
95   Turn from their office to black funeral—
Our instruments to melancholy bells,
Our wedding cheer to a sad burial feast;
Our solemn hymns to sullen dirges change;
Our bridal flowers serve for a buried corse;
100   And all things change them to the contrary.

Friar Laurence. Sir, go you in; and, madam, go with
him;
And go, Sir Paris. Every one prepare
To follow this fair corse unto her grave.
105   The heavens do lower upon you for some ill;

114-157 After the tragedy of Juliet's "death," Shakespeare injects a light and witty conversation between Peter and the musicians. Peter asks them to play "Heart's Ease," a popular song of the time and a **dump,** a sad song. They refuse, and insults and puns are traded. Peter says that instead of money he'll give them a jeering speech **(gleek),** and he insults them by calling them minstrels. In return they call him a servant. Then both make puns using notes of the singing scale, *re* and *fa*.

Move them no more by crossing their high will.

[Exeunt Capulet, Lady Capulet, Paris, and Friar.]

First Musician. Faith, we may put up our pipes, and be gone.

Nurse. Honest good fellows, ah, put up, put up,
110   For well you know this is a pitiful case.

[Exit.]

Second Musician. Aye, by my troth, the case may be amended.

[Enter Peter.]

Peter. Musicians, oh, musicians, "Heart's ease, heart's ease." Oh, an you will have me live, play "Heart's ease."

115 **First Musician.** Why "Heart's ease"?

Peter. Oh, musicians, because my heart itself plays "My heart is full of woe." Oh, play me some merry dump, to comfort me.

First Musician. Not a dump we, 'tis no time to play
120   now.

Peter. You will not, then?

First Musician. No.

Peter. I will then give it you soundly.

First Musician. What will you give us?

125 **Peter.** No money, on my faith, but the gleek. I will give you the minstrel.

First Musician. Then will I give you the serving creature.

Peter. Then will I lay the serving creature's dagger on
130   your pate. I will carry no crotchets. I'll re you, I'll fa you, do you note me?

First Musician. An you re us and fa us, you note us.

Second Musician. Pray you put up your dagger, and put out your wit.

135 **Peter.** Then have at you with my wit! I will drybeat you with an iron wit, and put up my iron dagger. Answer me like men:
    "When griping grief the heart doth wound
    And doleful dumps the mind oppress,
140   Then music with her silver sound—"
Why "silver sound"? Why "music with her silver sound"?—What say you, Simon Catling?

First Musician. Marry, sir, because silver hath a sweet sound.

145 **Peter.** Pretty! What say you, Hugh Rebeck?

Second Musician. I say "silver sound" because musicians sound for silver.

Peter. Pretty too! What say you, James Soundpost?

Third Musician. Faith, I know not what to say.

150 **Peter.** Oh, I cry you mercy, you are the singer. I will say for you. It is "music with her silver sound" because musicians have no gold for sounding.
    "Then music with her silver sound
    With speedy help doth lend redress."

[Exit.]

155 **First Musician.** What a pestilent knave is this same!

Second Musician. Hang him, Jack! Come, we'll in here. Tarry for the mourners, and stay dinner.

[Exeunt.]

1-5 If I can trust my dreams, something joyful is about to happen. My heart **(bosom's lord)** is happy and I am content.

6-10 *What was Romeo's dream?*

17 If Juliet is well, no news can be bad.

ACT FIVE

Scene 1 *A street in Mantua.*

*Balthasar, Romeo's servant, comes from
Verona to tell him that Juliet is dead and lies in
the Capulet's tomb. Since Romeo has not yet
received any word from the Friar, he believes
Balthasar. He immediately decides to return to
Verona in order to die next to Juliet. He sends
Balthasar away and sets out to find a pharma-
cist who will sell him poison.*

[Enter Romeo.]

Romeo. If I may trust the flattering truth of sleep,
My dreams presage some joyful news at hand.
My bosom's lord sits lightly in his throne,
And all this day an unaccustomed spirit
5   Lifts me above the ground with cheerful thoughts.
I dreamt my lady came and found me dead
(Strange dream that gives a dead man leave to
    think!)
And breathed such life with kisses in my lips
10   That I revived and was an emperor.
Ah me! how sweet is love itself possessed,
When but love's shadows are so rich in joy!

[Enter Romeo's servant, Balthasar, booted.]

News from Verona! How now, Balthasar?
Dost thou not bring me letters from the friar?
15   How doth my lady? Is my father well?
How fares my Juliet? That I ask again,
For nothing can be ill if she be well.

Balthasar. Then she is well, and nothing can be ill.

18-24 Balthasar replies that Juliet is well, since although her body is dead, her soul *(her immortal part)* is with the angels. As soon as he saw her in the tomb, he immediately rode to Mantua *(presently took post)* to tell Romeo. He asks forgiveness for bringing bad news but reminds Romeo that he had given Balthasar the duty *(office)* of bringing important news.

25 *I defy you, stars:* Romeo angrily challenges fate, which has caused him so much grief.

29-30 *import some misadventure:* suggest that something bad will happen.

37 *What does Romeo mean?*

38-43 *Let's see for means:* Let me find a way *(means)* to join Juliet in death. *apothecary:* pharmacist. *tattered weeds:* ragged clothes. *Culling of simples:* sorting herbs.

45-51 Romeo describes the items in the apothecary's shop.

52 *penury:* poverty.

Her body sleeps in Capels' monument,
20   And her immortal part with angels lives.
I saw her laid low in her kindred's vault
And presently took post to tell it you.
O, pardon me for bringing these ill news,
Since you did leave it for my office, sir.

25   **Romeo.** Is it e'en so? Then I defy you, stars!
Thou knowst my lodging. Get me ink and paper
And hire posthorses. I will hence tonight.

Balthasar. I do beseech you, sir, have patience
Your looks are pale and wild and do import
30   Some misadventure.

Romeo.   Tush, thou art deceived.
Leave me and do the thing I bid thee do.
Hast thou no letters to me from the friar?

Balthasar. No, my good lord.

35   **Romeo.**   No matter. Get thee gone
And hire those horses. I'll be with thee straight.

[Exit Balthasar.]

Well, Juliet, I will lie with thee tonight.
Let's see for means. O mischief, thou art swift
To enter in the thoughts of desperate men!
40   I do remember an apothecary,
And hereabouts he dwells, which late I noted
In tattered weeds, with overwhelming brows,
Culling of simples. Meager were his looks,
Sharp misery had worn him to the bones;
45   And in his needy shop a tortoise hung,
An alligator stuffed, and other skins
Of ill-shaped fishes; and about his shelves
A beggarly account of empty boxes,
Green earthen pots, bladders, and musty seeds,
50   Remnants of packthread, and old cakes of roses
Were thinly scattered, to make up a show.
Noting this penury, to myself I said,

53-55 Although it is a crime to sell poison, the apothecary is such a miserable person *(caitiff wretch)* that he would probably do it for the money.

63-69 *ducats:* gold coins. Forty ducats was a large sum of money. Romeo asks for fast-acting *(soon-speeding)* poison.

70-72 *Such . . . them:* I have such deadly drugs, but selling them is a crime punishable by death.

73-79 Romeo argues that the man lives in such misery he has no reason to fear death or the law. He urges the apothecary to improve his situation by selling the poison.

80 I'm doing this for the money, not because I think it's right.

81 I'm not paying your conscience.

84 *dispatch you straight:* kill you instantly.

"An if a man did need a poison now
Whose sale is present death in Mantua,
55   Here lives a caitiff wretch would sell it him."
O, this same thought did but forerun my need,
And this same needy man must sell it me.
As I remember, this should be the house.
Being holiday, the beggar's shop is shut.
60   What, ho! apothecary!

[Enter Apothecary.]

Apothecary. Who calls so loud?

Romeo. Come hither, man. I see that thou art poor.
Hold, there is forty ducats. Let me have
A dram of poison, such soon-speeding gear
65   As will disperse itself through all the veins
That the life-weary taker may fall dead,
And that the trunk may be discharged of breath
As violently as hasty powder fired
Doth hurry from the fatal cannon's womb.

70 **Apothecary.** Such mortal drugs I have; but
        Mantua's law
    Is death to any he that utters them.

Romeo. Art thou so bare and full of wretchedness
And fearest to die? Famine is in thy cheeks,
75   Need and oppression starveth in thine eyes,
Contempt and beggary hangs upon thy back:
The world is not thy friend, nor the world's law;
The world affords no law to make thee rich;
Then be not poor, but break it and take this.

80 **Apothecary.** My poverty but not my will consents.

Romeo. I pay thy poverty and not thy will.

Apothecary. Put this in any liquid thing you will
And drink it off, and if you had the strength
Of twenty men, it would dispatch you straight.

92 Romeo refers to the poison as a ***cordial,*** a drink believed to be good for the heart.

6-13 Friar John explains why he didn't go to Mantua. He had asked another friar ***(One of our order),*** who had been caring for the sick, to go with him. The health officials of the town, believing that the friars had come into contact with the deadly disease, the plague ***(infectious pestilence),*** locked them up to keep them from infecting others.

Act 5, scene 2

85 **Romeo.** There is thy gold—worse poison to men's
souls,
Doing more murder in this loathsome world,
Than these poor compounds that thou mayst
not sell.
90 I sell thee poison; thou hast sold me none.
Farewell. Buy food and get thyself in flesh.
Come, cordial and not poison, go with me
To Juliet's grave; for there must I use thee.

[Exeunt.]

Scene 2 *Friar Laurence's cell in Verona.*

*Friar Laurence's messenger arrives saying that
he was unable to deliver the letter to Romeo.
Friar Laurence, his plans ruined, rushes to the
Capulet vault before Juliet awakes. He intends
to hide her in his room until Romeo can come
to take her away.*

[Verona. Friar Laurence's cell.]

[Enter Friar John.]

Friar John. Holy Franciscan friar, brother, ho!

[Enter Friar Laurence.]

Friar Laurence. This same should be the voice of
Friar John.
Welcome from Mantua. What says Romeo?
5 Or, if his mind be writ, give me his letter.

Friar John. Going to find a barefoot brother out,
One of our order to associate me,
Here in this city visiting the sick,
And finding him, the searchers of the town,
10 Suspecting that we both were in a house
Where the infectious pestilence did reign,
Sealed up the doors, and would not let us forth,

The Tragedy of Romeo and Juliet **213**

14 *bare:* carried (bore).

19-21 The letter wasn't trivial *(nice)* but rather contained instructions *(charge)* of great importance *(dear import).* The fact that it wasn't sent *(neglecting it)* may cause great harm. *What would the letter have told Romeo that he does not know?*

22 *iron crow:* crowbar. *Why might Friar Laurence need a crowbar?*

25-28 Now I must hurry to Juliet's side, since she'll awaken in three hours. Juliet will be furious with me *(beshrew me)* when she discovers that Romeo doesn't know what has happened.

So that my speed to Mantua there was stayed.

Friar Laurence. Who bare my letter, then, to Romeo?

15 **Friar John.** I could not send it—here it is again—
Nor get a messenger to bring it thee,
So fearful were they of infection.

Friar Laurence. Unhappy fortune! By my brotherhood,
The letter was not nice, but full of charge,
20 Of dear import, and the neglecting it
May do much danger. Friar John, go hence,
Get me an iron crow and bring it straight
Unto my cell.

Friar John.   Brother, I'll go and bring it thee.

[Exit.]

25 **Friar Laurence.** Now must I to the monument alone.
Within this three hours will fair Juliet wake.
She will beshrew me much that Romeo
Hath had no notice of these accidents;
But I will write again to Mantua,
30 And keep her at my cell till Romeo come—
Poor living corse, closed in a dead man's tomb!

[Exeunt.]

1-9 Paris wants nobody to know that he is visiting Juliet's tomb. He tells his servant to keep his ear to the ground and whistle if anyone comes near.

Scene 3 *The cemetery that contains the Capulets' tomb.*

*In the dark of night Paris comes to the
cemetery to put flowers on Juliet's grave. At
the same time Romeo arrives, and Paris hides.
Romeo opens the tomb and Paris assumes that
he is going to harm the bodies. He challenges
Romeo, who warns him to leave. They fight
and Romeo kills Paris. When Romeo recognizes
the dead Paris, he lays his body inside the tomb
as Paris requested. Romeo declares his love for
Juliet, drinks the poison, and dies. Shortly after,
Friar Laurence arrives and discovers both
bodies. When Juliet wakes up, the Friar urges
her to leave with him before the guard comes.
Juliet refuses and when the Friar leaves, she
kills herself with Romeo's dagger. The guards
and the Prince arrive, followed by the Capulets
and Lord Montague, whose wife has just died
because of Romeo's exile. Friar Laurence and
both servants explain what has happened.
Capulet and Montague finally end their feud
and promise to erect statues honoring Romeo
and Juliet.*

[Enter Paris and his Page with flowers and a torch.]

Paris. Give me thy torch, boy. Hence, and stand aloof.
Yet put it out, for I would not be seen.
Under yond yew tree lay thee all along,
Holding thine ear close to the hollow ground.
5   So shall no foot upon the churchyard tread
(Being loose, unfirm, with digging up of graves)
But thou shalt hear it. Whistle then to me,
As signal that thou hearst something approach.
Give me those flowers. Do as I bid thee, go.

10 **Page.** *[Aside]* I am almost afraid to stand alone
Here in the churchyard; yet I will adventure.

[Withdraws.]

12-17 Paris promises to decorate Juliet's grave with flowers, as he does now, and with either perfume *(sweet water)* or his tears. He will perform these honoring rites *(obsequies)* every night.

19-22 *What cursed . . . awhile:* who dares to interrupt my ritual? Is he even carrying a torch? Let the darkness hide me. *mattock . . . iron:* ax and crowbar.

23-24 *What might Romeo have written to his father?*

28-32 *What two reasons does Romeo give for going into Juliet's tomb?*

32 *In dear employment:* for an important purpose.

33-39 Romeo threatens that if Balthasar returns because he is curious *(jealous),* Romeo will rip him apart and throw his bones around the churchyard. His intention is more unstoppable *(inexorable)* than a hungry *(empty)* tiger or the waves of an ocean.

Paris. Sweet flower, with flowers thy bridal bed I strew

[He strews the tomb with flowers.]

    (O woe! thy canopy is dust and stones)
    Which with sweet water nightly I will dew;
15   Or, wanting that, with tears distilled by moans.
    The obsequies that I for thee will keep
    Nightly shall be to strew thy grave and weep.

[The Page *whistles.]*

    The boy gives warning something doth approach.
    What cursed foot wanders this way tonight
20   To cross my obsequies and true love's rite?
    What, with a torch? Muffle me, night, awhile.

[Withdraws.]

[Enter Romeo *and* Balthasar *with a torch, a mattock, and a crow of iron.]*

Romeo. Give me that mattock and the wrenching iron.
    Hold, take this letter. Early in the morning
    See thou deliver it to my lord and father.
25   Give me the light. Upon thy life I charge thee,
    Whate'er thou hearest or seest, stand all aloof
    And do not interrupt me in my course.
    Why I descend into this bed of death
    Is partly to behold my lady's face,
30   But chiefly to take thence from her dead finger
    A precious ring—a ring that I must use
    In dear employment. Therefore hence, be gone.
    But if thou, jealous, dost return to pry
    In what I farther shall intend to do,
35   By heaven, I will tear thee joint by joint
    And strew this hungry churchyard with thy limbs.
    The time and my intents are savage-wild,
    More fierce and more inexorable far
    Than empty tigers or the roaring sea.

40 **Balthasar.** I will be gone, sir, and not trouble you.

44-45 Balthasar decides to hide in the cemetery in spite of what he has just promised Romeo. *Who else is hiding in the cemetery at this point?*

47-50 Romeo addresses the tomb as though it were devouring people. He calls it a hateful stomach *(detestable maw)* that is filled *(gorged)* with the dearest morsel of earth, Juliet. He uses his crowbar to open its *rotten jaws* and feeds himself to it.

55-59 *apprehend:* arrest. Recognizing Romeo, Paris speaks these lines to himself. He is angry with Romeo, believing that Romeo's having killed Tybalt caused Juliet to die of grief for her cousin. *What does he think Romeo intends to do at the tomb?*

60-69 Romeo rejects Paris' challenge. He tells Paris to think of those already killed and leave before Romeo is forced to kill him too. Romeo swears that he has come to harm himself, not Paris.

70-71 I reject your appeal *(defy thy conjuration)* and arrest you as a criminal.

Romeo. So shalt thou show me friendship. Take thou
    that.
  Live, and be prosperous; and farewell, good fellow.

Balthasar. *[Aside]* For all this same, I'll hide me
45   hereabout.
  His looks I fear, and his intents I doubt.

[Withdraws.]

Romeo. Thou detestable maw, thou womb of death,
  Gorged with the dearest morsel of the earth,
  Thus I enforce thy rotten jaws to open,
50 And in despite I'll cram thee with more food.

[Romeo opens the tomb.]

Paris. This is that banisht haughty Montague
  That murdered my love's cousin—with which grief
  It is supposed the fair creature died—
  And here is come to do some villainous shame
55 To the dead bodies. I will apprehend him.
  Stop thy unhallowed toil, vile Montague!
  Can vengeance be pursued further than death?
  Condemned villain, I do apprehend thee.
  Obey, and go with me; for thou must die.

60 **Romeo.** I must indeed; and therefore came I hither.
  Good gentle youth, tempt not a desp'rate man.
  Fly hence and leave me. Think upon these gone;
  Let them affright thee. I beseech thee, youth,
  Put not another sin upon my head
65 By urging me to fury. O, be gone!
  By heaven, I love thee better than myself.
  For I come hither armed against myself.
  Stay not, be gone. Live, and hereafter say
  A madman's mercy bid thee run away.

70 **Paris.** I do defy thy conjuration
  And apprehend thee for a felon here.

77-90 Romeo discovers that the man he has just killed is Paris, whom he vaguely remembers was supposed to marry Juliet. He says that like himself, Paris has been a victim of bad luck. He will bury him with Juliet, whose beauty fills the tomb with light. Paris' corpse **(Death)** is being buried **(interred)** by a dead man in that Romeo expects to be dead soon.

95-99 Romeo notices that death has had no effect on Juliet's beauty. The sign **(ensign)** of beauty is still in Juliet's red lips and rosy cheeks.

Romeo. Wilt thou provoke me? Then have at
  thee, boy!

[They fight.]

Page. O Lord, they fight! I will go call the watch.

[Exit.]

75 **Paris.** O, I am slain! *[Falls.]* If thou be merciful,
  Open the tomb, lay me with Juliet.

[Dies.]

Romeo. In faith, I will. Let me peruse this face.
  Mercutio's kinsman, noble County Paris!
  What said my man when my betossed soul
80 Did not attend him as we rode? I think
  He told me Paris should have married Juliet.
  Said he not so? or did I dream it so?
  Or am I mad, hearing him talk of Juliet,
  To think it was so? O, give me thy hand,
85 One writ with me in sour misfortune's book!
  I'll bury thee in a triumphant grave.
  A grave? O, no, a lantern, slaughtered youth,
  For here lies Juliet, and her beauty makes
  This vault a feasting presence full of light.
90 Death, lie thou there, by a dead man interred.

[Lays Paris in the tomb.]

  How oft when men are at the point of death
  Have they been merry! which their keepers call
  A lightning before death. O, how may I
  Call this a lightning? O my love! my wife!
95 Death, that hath sucked the honey of thy breath,
  Hath had no power yet upon thy beauty.
  Thou art not conquered. Beauty's ensign yet
  Is crimson in thy lips and in thy cheeks,
  And death's pale flag is not advanced there.
100 Tybalt, liest thou there in thy bloody sheet?
  O, what more favor can I do to thee

101-103 ***O, what . . . enemy:*** I can best repay you (Tybalt) by
killing your enemy (myself) with the same hand that
cut your youth in two ***(twain).***

105-108 Romeo can't get over how beautiful Juliet still looks.
He asks whether Death is loving ***(amorous)*** and
whether it has taken Juliet as its lover ***(paramour).***

112-115 ***O, here . . . flesh:*** Here I will cause my death
(everlasting rest) and rid myself of the burden
(shake the yoke) of an unhappy fate ***(inauspicious
stars).***

118 ***dateless:*** eternal; neverending. Romeo means that
what he is about to do can never be undone.

120-121 ***thy seasick weary bark:*** Romeo compares himself to
the pilot of a ship ***(bark)*** who is going to crash on the
rocks because he is so weary and sick.

Than with that hand that cut thy youth in twain
To sunder his that was thine enemy?
Forgive me, cousin! Ah, dear Juliet,
105 Why art thou yet so fair? Shall I believe
That unsubstantial Death is amorous,
And that the lean abhorred monster keeps
Thee here in dark to be his paramour?
For fear of that I still will stay with thee
110 And never from this palace of dim night
Depart again. Here, here will I remain
With worms that are thy chambermaids. O, here
Will I set up my everlasting rest
And shake the yoke of inauspicious stars
115 From this world-wearied flesh. Eyes, look your last!
Arms, take your last embrace! and, lips, O you
The doors of breath, seal with a righteous kiss
A dateless bargain to engrossing death!
Come, bitter conduct; come, unsavory guide!
120 Thou desperate pilot, now at once run on
The dashing rocks thy seasick weary bark!
Here's to my love! *[Drinks.]* O true apothecary!
Thy drugs are quick. Thus with a kiss I die.

[Falls.]

[Enter Friar Laurence, *with lantern, crow, and spade.]*

Friar Laurence. Saint Francis be my speed! how
125   oft tonight
Have my old feet stumbled at graves! Who's there?

Balthasar. Here's one, a friend, and one that knows
you well.

Friar Laurence. Bliss be upon you! Tell me, good
130   my friend,
What torch is yond that vainly lends his light
To grubs and eyeless skulls? As I discern,
It burneth in the Capels' monument.

141-144 I can't go with you to the tomb. My master threatened me with death if I stayed here.

145-147 The Friar fears that something unlucky *(unthrifty)* has happened.

151-155 Why are these bloody swords lying here at the tomb *(sepulcher),* a place that should be peaceful? (The swords are also *masterless,* or without their owners.)

Balthasar. It doth so, holy sir; and there's my master,
135   One that you love.

Friar Laurence. Who is it?

Balthasar.   Romeo.

Friar Laurence. How long hath he been there?

Balthasar. Full half an hour.

140 **Friar Laurence.** Go with me to the vault.

Balthasar.   I dare not, sir.
    My master knows not but I am gone hence,
    And fearfully did menace me with death
    If I did stay to look on his intents.

145 **Friar Laurence.** Stay then; I'll go alone. Fear comes
      upon me.
    O, much I fear some ill unthrifty thing.

Balthasar. As I did sleep under this yew tree here,
    I dreamt my master and another fought,
150   And that my master slew him.

Friar Laurence.   Romeo!

[Stoops and looks on the blood and weapons.]

    Alack, alack, what blood is this which stains
    The stony entrance of this sepulcher?
    What mean these masterless and gory swords
155   To lie discolored by this place of peace?

[Enters the tomb.]

    Romeo! O, pale! Who else? What, Paris too?
    And steeped in blood? Ah, what an unkind hour
    Is guilty of this lamentable chance!
    The lady stirs.

160 *comfortable:* comforting.

163-173 The Friar hears noise and wants Juliet to get out of the awful tomb. He says that a greater force than they can fight *(contradict),* meaning God or fate, has ruined their plans *(thwarted our intents).* He informs her of Romeo's and Paris' deaths and says he'll find a place for her in a convent of nuns. *Why is the Friar so anxious to leave?*

175 *timeless:* happening before its proper time.

176-180 Juliet calls Romeo a miser *(churl)* for not leaving some poison for her. She kisses him, hoping that perhaps *(haply)* some of the poison is still on his lips.

183 From this point on, the churchyard will be filled with people and lights.

[Juliet *rises.*]

160 **Juliet.** O comfortable friar! where is my lord?
I do remember well where I should be,
And there I am. Where is my Romeo?

Friar Laurence. I hear some noise. Lady, come from
that nest

165 Of death, contagion, and unnatural sleep.
A greater power than we can contradict
Hath thwarted our intents. Come, come away.
Thy husband in thy bosom there lies dead;
And Paris too. Come, I'll dispose of thee

170 Among a sisterhood of holy nuns.
Stay not to question, for the watch is coming.
Come, go, good Juliet. I dare no longer stay.

Juliet. Go, get thee hence, for I will not away.

[Exit Friar Laurence.]

What's here? A cup, closed in my true love's hand?
175 Poison, I see, hath been his timeless end.
O churl! drunk all, and left no friendly drop
To help me after? I will kiss thy lips.
Haply some poison yet doth hang on them
To make me die with a restorative.

[Kisses him.]

180 Thy lips are warm!

Chief Watchman. [Within] Lead, boy. Which way?

Juliet. Yea, noise? Then I'll be brief. O happy dagger!

[Snatches Romeo's dagger.]

This is thy sheath; there rust, and let me die.

[She stabs herself and falls.]

[Enter Watchmen with the Page of Paris.]

Page. This is the place. There, where the torch doth
185 burn.

188 *attach:* arrest.

193 *Raise up:* awaken.

194-196 We see the earth *(ground)* these bodies lie on. But the real cause *(true ground)* of these deaths is yet for us to discover *(descry).*

199-205 The guards arrest Balthasar and Friar Laurence as suspicious characters.

Chief Watchman. The ground is bloody. Search about
    the churchyard.
    Go, some of you; whoe'er you find attach.

[Exeunt some of the Watch.]

    Pitiful sight! here lies the County slain;
190   And Juliet bleeding, warm, and newly dead,
    Who here hath lain this two days buried.
    Go, tell the Prince; run to the Capulets;
    Raise up the Montagues; some others search.

[Exeunt others of the Watch.]

    We see the ground whereon these woes do lie,
195   But the true ground of all these piteous woes
    We cannot without circumstance descry.

[Reenter some of the Watch, with Balthasar.]

Second Watchman. Here's Romeo's man. We found
    him in the churchyard.

Chief Watchman. Hold him in safety till the Prince
200   come hither.

[Reenter Friar Laurence and another Watchman.]

Third Watchman. Here is a friar that trembles, sighs,
    and weeps.
    We took this mattock and this spade from him
    As he was coming from this churchyard side.

205 **Chief Watchman.** A great suspicion! Stay the friar too.

[Enter the Prince and Attendants.]

Prince. What misadventure is so early up,
    That calls our person from our morning rest?

[Enter Capulet, Lady Capulet, and others.]

Capulet. What should it be, that they so shriek abroad?

212 *startles:* causes alarm.

225-227 This dagger has missed its target. It should rest in the sheath *(house)* that Romeo wears. Instead it is in Juliet's bosom.

232-234 My son's exile has caused my wife to die. What other sadness plots against me in my old age?

236-237 *what manners . . . grave:* What kind of behavior is this, for a son to die before his father?

238-245 *Seal . . . descent:* Stop your emotional outbursts until we can find out the source *(spring)* of these confusing events *(ambiguities).* Wait *(forbear)* and let's find out what happened.

Lady Capulet. The people in the street cry "Romeo,"
210   Some "Juliet," and some "Paris"; and all run,
     With open outcry, toward our monument.

Prince. What fear is this which startles in our ears?

Chief Watchman. Sovereign, here lies the County
     Paris slain;   215   And Romeo dead,
     and Juliet, dead before,
     Warm and new killed.

Prince. Search, seek, and know how this foul
     murder comes.

Chief Watchman. Here is a friar, and slaughtered
220   Romeo's man,
     With instruments upon them fit to open
     These dead men's tombs.

Capulet. O heavens! O wife, look how our daughter
     bleeds!
225   This dagger hath mista'en, for, lo, his house
     Is empty on the back of Montague,
     And it missheathed in my daughter's bosom!

Lady Capulet. O me! this sight of death is as a bell
     That warns my old age to a sepulcher.

[Enter Montague and others.]

230 **Prince.** Come, Montague; for thou art early up
     To see thy son and heir now early down.

Montague. Alas, my liege, my wife is dead tonight!
     Grief of my son's exile hath stopped her breath.
     What further woe conspires against mine age?

235 **Prince.** Look, and thou shalt see.

Montague. O thou untaught! what manners is in this,
     To press before thy father to a grave?

Prince. Seal up the mouth of outrage for a while,
     Till we can clear these ambiguities

246-250 Friar Laurence confesses that he is most responsible for these events. He will both accuse *(impeach)* himself and clear *(purge)* himself of guilt.

259 It was Romeo's banishment, not Tybalt's death, that made Juliet sad.

272 *borrowed:* temporary.

240 And know their spring, their head, their true
     descent;
     And then will I be general of your woes
     And lead you even to death. Meantime forbear,
     And let mischance be slave to patience.
245 Bring forth the parties of suspicion.

Friar Laurence. I am the greatest, able to do least,
     Yet most suspected, as the time and place
     Doth make against me, of this direful murder;
     And here I stand, both to impeach and purge
250 Myself condemned and myself excused.

Prince. Then say at once what thou dost know in this.

Friar Laurence. I will be brief, for my short date
     of breath
     Is not so long as is a tedious tale.
255 Romeo, there dead, was husband to that Juliet;
     And she, there dead, that Romeo's faithful wife.
     I married them; and their stol'n marriage day
     Was Tybalt's doomsday, whose untimely death
     Banisht the new-made bridegroom from this city;
260 For whom, and not for Tybalt, Juliet pined.
     You, to remove that siege of grief from her,
     Betrothed and would have married her perforce
     To County Paris. Then comes she to me
     And with wild looks bid me devise some mean
265 To rid her from this second marriage,
     Or in my cell there would she kill herself.
     Then gave I her (so tutored by my art)
     A sleeping potion; which so took effect
     As I intended, for it wrought on her
270 The form of death. Meantime I writ to Romeo
     That he should hither come as this dire night
     To help to take her from her borrowed grave,
     Being the time the potion's force should cease.
     But he which bore my letter, Friar John,
275 Was stayed by accident, and yesternight
     Returned my letter back. Then all alone

289-293 ***and to . . . law:*** Her nurse can bear witness to the secret marriage. If I am responsible for any of this, let the law punish me with death.

297 ***in post:*** at full speed.

303-304 ***Where . . . this place:*** The Prince asks for Paris' servant, who notified the guards ***(raised the watch).*** Then he asks the servant why Paris was at the cemetery.

307-309 Soon ***(Anon),*** someone with a light came and opened the tomb. Paris drew his sword, and I ran to call the guards.

310 Romeo's letter shows that Friar Laurence has told the truth.

At the prefixed hour of her waking
Came I to take her from her kindred's vault;
Meaning to keep her closely at my cell
280 Till I conveniently could send to Romeo.
But when I came, some minute ere the time
Of her awaking, here untimely lay
The noble Paris and true Romeo dead.
She wakes; and I entreated her come forth
285 And bear this work of heaven with patience;
But then a noise did scare me from the tomb,
And she, too desperate, would not go with me,
But, as it seems, did violence on herself.
All this I know, and to the marriage
290 Her nurse is privy; and if aught in this
Miscarried by my fault, let my old life
Be sacrificed, some hour before his time,
Unto the rigor of severest law.

Prince. We still have known thee for a holy man.
295 Where's Romeo's man? What can he say in this?

Balthasar. I brought my master news of Juliet's death;
And then in post he came from Mantua
To this same place, to this same monument.
This letter he early bid me give his father,
300 And threatened me with death, going in the vault,
If I departed not and left him there.

Prince. Give me the letter. I will look on it.
Where is the County's page that raised the watch?
Sirrah, what made your master in this place?

305 **Page.** He came with flowers to strew his lady's grave;
And bid me stand aloof, and so I did.
Anon comes one with light to ope the tomb;
And by-and-by my master drew on him;
And then I ran away to call the watch.

310 **Prince.** This letter doth make good the friar's words,
Their course of love, the tidings of her death;
And here he writes that he did buy a poison

315-319 Where are the enemies whose feud started all this trouble? Capulet and Montague, look at the punishment your hatred has brought on you. Heaven has killed your children **(joys)** with love. For shutting my eyes to your arguments **(discords),** I have lost two relatives (Mercutio and Paris). We all have been punished.

321 **jointure:** dowry, the payment a bride's father makes to the groom. Capulet means that no one could demand more of a bride's father than he has already paid.

324-327 **at such rate be set:** be valued so highly. *What does Montague promise to do for the memory of Juliet?*

328-329 Capulet promises to do the same for Romeo as Montague will do for Juliet. Their children have become sacrifices to their hatred **(enmity).**

Of a poor 'pothecary, and therewithal
Came to this vault to die and lie with Juliet.
315 Where be these enemies? Capulet, Montague,
See what a scourge is laid upon your hate,
That heaven finds means to kill your joys with love!
And I, for winking at your discords too,
Have lost a brace of kinsmen. All are punished.

320 **Capulet.** O brother Montague, give me thy hand.
This is my daughter's jointure, for no more
Can I demand.

Montague.   But I can give thee more;
For I will raise her statue in pure gold,
325 That whiles Verona by that name is known,
There shall no figure at such rate be set
As that of true and faithful Juliet.

Capulet. As rich shall Romeo's by his lady's lie—
Poor sacrifices of our enmity!

330 **Prince.** A glooming peace this morning with it brings.
The sun for sorrow will not show his head.
Go hence, to have more talk of these sad things;
Some shall be pardoned, and some punished;
For never was a story of more woe
335 Than this of Juliet and her Romeo.

[Exeunt.]

RELATED READINGS

from Twisted Tales from Shakespeare

by Richard Armour

How would you recount the events of Romeo and Juliet *to a friend? In this humorous essay, Armour spoofs Shakespeare's drama and provides extra details to enliven this classic story of young love.*

Introduction

The plot of *Romeo and Juliet* came to England from Italy through France, arriving tired and dusty and covered with hotel stickers. Passed from person to person by word of mouth, it picked up interesting details and several of the more popular diseases of the sixteenth century. As with most of Shakespeare's works, scholars believe this also was preceded by a lost play. Elizabethans never could remember where they left things.

Romeo and Juliet is one of Shakespeare's early works. Microscopic examination of the First Quarto (Q1) reveals no trace of hair, and leads to the assumption that the play was written before Shakespeare grew a beard.[1] It unquestionably, perhaps even indubitably, belongs to that period of Shakespeare's life when he was experimenting with

---

1. The First Quarto is known as a "bad" quarto, although we are not told what it did to get this reputation.

lyricism. The verse has a fluid quality, purple splotches being interspersed with brown puddles where the author gave way to his weakness for liquid syllables.

The style in general is marked by numerous figures of speech—metaphors, semaphors, twongue-tisters, etc. An occasional wordy passage is offset by a passage of equal length in which Shakespeare strips his language bare and uses no words whatsoever. The stark simplicity of these latter passages beggars description.[2]

Shakespeare represents the love of Romeo and Juliet as that of two young people caught in the toils of Fate and unable to help themselves. In that hot Italian summer, passions were high and shirts were damp. Both of the lovers grow in stature as the story unfolds, until by the last act Romeo stands well over six feet in his sandals and Juliet has to let down the hem of her kirtle. At the beginning of the play Romeo and Juliet are callow and impetuous; by the end of the play they are noble, dignified, and dead.

Romeo and Juliet has long been one of the most popular of Shakespeare's plays, enjoyed especially by young people who identify themselves with the two lovers[3] and by poets who identify themselves with Shakespeare. The balcony scene has been played all over the world, except possibly in regions where there are only one-story houses. If the part of Juliet has sometimes overshadowed that of Romeo, it is because Romeo spends so much time under the balcony.

2. And, if long continued, might have impoverished the author.
3. Young men tend to identify themselves with Romeo and young women with Juliet.

A family feud

The play opens with a Prologue which tells the whole story and makes it unnecessary to go any further.[4] It seems that in the Italian city of Verona a feud is going on between the Montagues and the Capulets, it being the height of the feudal period. What made the Montagues mad at the Capulets and vice versa is not explained. Evidently it's something that happened so long ago that nobody can remember, like Yale and Harvard. Anyhow, there's no feud like an old feud, and no one likes to upset a Tradition.

Since the Montagues and the Capulets carry swords and fight at the drop of a pizza, those red spots on the pavement really *are* blood. Hot-headed young fellows are always running swords through one another. "Draw!" they shout, which is the signal to pull their swords out of each other and look to see who made the larger hole.

Escalus, the Prince of Verona, is getting sick of all this bloodshed. Every time someone is killed, he loses a taxpayer.

"What, ho! you men, you beasts," he cries, making sure to include everyone. He warns Montague and Capulet that this brawling has to stop, or they will forfeit their own lives. This puts a new complexion on things.[5]

"If there is any fighting from now on," Montague and Capulet promise, "it will be over our dead bodies." Escalus nods approvingly.

---

4. Anyone continuing is warned to look out for "the two hours' traffic of our stage," with dozens of Italians careening crazily to and from the wings.
5. I.e., they turn pale.

Romeo meets Juliet

Romeo, the son of Montague, is a handsome young fellow who is in an advanced stage of lovesickness for a girl named Rosaline. He sighs all day long, and is getting short of breath.[6] At night he can hardly wait to get to sleep so he can start dreaming. But Rosaline cares for him not a whit.

Hoping to make him forget Rosaline, two swashbuckling friends of his, Benvolio and Mercutio, persuade him to crash a party at the Capulets'. Since Romeo and Benvolio are Montagues, they don masks, hoping to be mistaken for burglars.

Old Capulet's daughter, Juliet, is the most luscious damsel at the party. When Romeo casts eyes on her, she playfully tosses them back. He feels an electric shock run through him, even though the place is lit by torches, and forgets Rosaline completely.[7]

"It seems she hangs upon the cheek of night like a rich jewel in an Ethiop's ear," remarks Romeo, who is a quick man with a simile, no matter how ridiculous. In a short while he has made her acquaintance, and before the evening is over has worked up to a kiss.[8]

"You kiss by the book," Juliet comments. Seems she has read the same how-to opus and recognizes the system. She puckers up again, ready to move on to the next chapter.

Tybalt, a young Capulet who hates the Montagues' guts, which he is always spilling into the gutter,

---

6. "Love is a smoke raised with the fume of sighs," he says, his head in the clouds.
7. In fact the poor girl is never heard of again, thus missing her chance for immortality in what might have been Shakespeare's *Romeo and Rosaline*.
8. He worked up from her neck to her lips, and hoped he hadn't gone too far.

recognizes Romeo by the way he smacks his lips.

"Fetch me my rapier, boy," he says to his caddy, passing up his broadsword and his eight iron. He is about to run Romeo through when he is stopped by old Capulet.

"Let him alone," Capulet says brusquely. Then, when Tybalt tries to argue, he shouts, "Go to!" Tybalt goes, although his destination is unspecified.[9]

At last Juliet's mother calls her, and Juliet withdraws.[10]

Later that night Romeo learns from Benvolio that Juliet is a Capulet, and Juliet learns from her nanny that Romeo is a Montague.

"I love a loathèd enemy," says Juliet, who is only fourteen and a crazy, mixed-up Capulet.

As for Romeo, despite all that osculation he's none too sure of himself. After all, Juliet has never seen him without his mask on.

Romeo goes back for more

Later that night Romeo gives his friends the slip and climbs over the wall into the Capulets' orchard. ("Leaps the wall," the text says, but Shakespeare was inclined to exaggerate.) He has a wonderful chance to purloin some fruit, but passes it up when he sees Juliet standing on her bedroom balcony in her negligee, looking neglegected. At sight of her, Romeo goes slightly daft, mumbling about putting her eyes in the sky and replacing them with stars, probably two of the smaller ones.

9. Shakespeare's two favorite devices for removing characters from the stage are "exeunts" and "go to's."
10. Her lips.

"O that I were a glove[11] upon that hand, that I might touch that cheek!" he exclaims, getting more and more impractical.

Juliet, who has an extraordinary sense of smell, realizes that Romeo is in the vicinity. "O Romeo, Romeo!" (probably a misreading of "Aromeo, aromeo") she cries out. "Wherefore art thou at, Romeo?" And then, lest he take offense, she hastily adds, "A rose by any other name would smell as sweet."

As Romeo gazes hungrily at her, Juliet becomes embarrassed. "Thou know'st the mask of night is on my face," she explains, chagrined at being caught with her cold cream on. But in the pale moonlight, Romeo seems not to have noticed this.

They converse until almost morning, Juliet leaning from her balcony and Romeo pacing about underneath. At last she retires, chilled to the bone, and Romeo goes home with a crick in his neck.

Romeo and Juliet elope

Early the next morning Romeo calls on his friend, Friar Laurence, who is already up and puttering about in his garden, gathering a basketful of weeds for breakfast. "O, mickle is the powerful grace that lies in plants, herbs, stones," he mutters to himself as he works. Mickle, it appears, is a rare substance, rich in vitamins.

"Good morrow, Father," Romeo greets him casually, as if he too were an early riser instead of one who hasn't been to bed. Forthwith he asks the priest to arrange a little marriage ceremony. When Friar Laurence learns that the bride-to-be is Juliet, he is delighted, it being something of a feather in his

11. In view of Juliet's age, it would have to be a kid glove.

tonsure to marry a Montague and a Capulet.

At this point the plot is considerably helped by Juliet's nurse, a talkative old Cupidess who is always shuffling on and off stage, carrying notes. Apparently she is a practical nurse, with a special permit from the Postal Department.

Thanks to her efforts, Juliet meets Romeo at Friar Laurence's cell and they become mates.[12] Getting married in those days was simple. There were no questionnaires, no blood tests, no fingerprints. Moreover, a minor like Juliet didn't have to get her parents' consent, which was a good thing in this instance.

Juliet, now Mrs. R. Montague, goes back to her balcony. The nurse smuggles in a rope ladder which will be dropped that night as soon as Romeo arrives with a new soliloquy. It's not the most auspicious beginning for a marriage, but Romeo will soon be learning the ropes.

Some unfortunate swordplay

Tybalt, a hot-headed Capulet, is spoiling for a fight. It's a warm day, and, with no refrigeration, nothing keeps very well. Meeting Benvolio and Mercutio in the public square, Tybalt stands fast[13] and exchanges insults with them, at the current rate. But he is really much more interested in insulting Romeo, who at this moment arrives.

"Thou art a villain," Tybalt snarls unsmilingly. This is pretty strong language, and Romeo should take umbrage.[14] But, remembering that he is now related to Tybalt by marriage, he replies politely. He realizes that you have to put up with a good deal from in-laws.

12. Cellmates.
13. This is done by marking time at the double.
14. Perhaps he does, deep down inside where it isn't visible.

"Tybalt, you rat-catcher!"[15] Mercutio says colorfully, whipping out his sword.

"I am for you!" cries Tybalt, trying to mix him up, really being against him.

As they fight, Romeo steps between them, his courage matched only by his stupidity. Tybalt thrusts under Romeo's arm and stabs Mercutio and flies. We are not told what happened to the flies, but Mercutio is in a bad way.

"I am hurt," he groans, in one of the greatest understatements in all Shakespeare.

"Courage, man, the hurt cannot be much," says Romeo, who fails to notice that his friend is standing up to his ankles in blood.

Not until Mercutio is dead does Romeo appreciate the seriousness of the situation. Then he vows to get back at Tybalt[16] for his underhanded underarm thrust. Completely forgetting about Tybalt's being a relative on his wife's side, Romeo unsheathes, feints, parries, and thrusts. "Tybalt falls," we are told, and in a Shakespearean tragedy this usually means he is dead, which turns out to be the case.

Romeo could be executed for this act of passion, but Benvolio pleads with the Prince, who lets Romeo off easy, merely banishing him for life. To a home-town boy, who believes there is no place like Verona, this is the end.[17]

15. The equivalent of the modern dog-catcher, or man-with-the-net. Anyhow, it's good to know that Tybalt is employed.
16. Who has returned to the scene, probably to retrieve his sword, which he left sticking in Mercutio.
17. There are, however, three and a half acts still to come.

Things are a mess

That night Juliet is waiting impatiently for Romeo to come climbing up the rope, hand over hand, and ready to hand over herself. She thinks happily of their life together, and dreams up an unusual way to memorialize her husband.

"When he shall die," she muses sentimentally, "take him and cut him out in little stars."[18] I Apparently she can see herself with a cookie cutter, and bits of Romeo all over the place. She has quite an imagination.

Just then the Nurse arrives with the news that Romeo has killed her kinsman, Tybalt, and been banished. At first Juliet shrieks piteously to learn that Tybalt has been slain, and by her husband of all people. She ransacks her vocabulary for suitable epithets to describe Romeo.

"O serpent heart, hid with a flowering face!" she screams, remembering the time he wriggled up the trellis with a long-stemmed rose in each nostril.

But her mood changes. A shudder goes through her frame. She blanches, clutches her breast, and staggers upstage left.

"Some word there was, worser than Tybalt's death," she says to the Nurse, lapsing into the grammar of her age.[19] Before the Nurse can tell her what it was, she remembers. It was "banished." The tears gush forth more violently than ever, but now in Romeo's direction. After all, she has several cousins but only one husband. Subsiding, Juliet tells the Nurse to give Romeo a ring. Since there are no telephones, the poor old soul has to shuffle the weary miles to Friar Laurence's cell, where Romeo is hiding.

18. See what Romeo wanted to do with Juliet's eyes. They both
    have star fixations.
19. Fourteen.

Romeo is blue about his banishment,[20] but cheers up when the Nurse arrives with word that Juliet still loves him, though he must promise never to do anything like that to Tybalt again. He is further cheered when the Friar says that if he will lie low in Mantua for a while, the news of his marriage can be broken gently to old Capulet, who will welcome his son-in-law back with open arms.[21] Friar Laurence is president of the Optimist Club of Verona.

Romeo returns for one almost idyllic night with Juliet before he hies himself to Mantua. It might have been perfect, indeed, but for a small disagreement. They hear a bird singing, and Juliet says it's a nightingale in a pomegranate tree, while Romeo insists it's a lark in the poison ivy. They argue about this until dawn, and Romeo might have been caught with his ladder down had not the Nurse come in.

"The day is broke," she announces, slaughtering the King's Italian. Romeo takes one last kiss (for the road) and is on his way to Mantua.

Just as things seem to be taking a turn for the better, Juliet gets some bad news. Her mother brings word that she is to marry the County Paris next Thursday.

Juliet is aghast, and feels very little better when she learns that County Paris is only one man. She vows she will not marry him, come Hell or high water, both of which at the moment seem unlikely. What does come is her father, old Capulet, and when he hears that Juliet won't have Paris, he is furious.

"You baggage!" he cries, swearing he will put handles on her and carry her to church himself, if

---

20. And not helped any by the good Friar's remark, "Thou art wedded to calamity," a tactless thing to say to a bridegroom, whatever he may think of the bride.
21. Firearms, perhaps.

necessary. Then he gets even uglier. "I will drag thee on a hurdle thither."[22]

"Fie, fie!" interjects Lady Capulet, whose language is refined and monosyllabic.

"You green-sickness carrion! You tallow-face!"[23] Capulet shouts, reaching a crescendo of paternal enthusiasm, and more than a little proud of his vocabulary. "Fettle your fine joints 'gainst Thursday next," he says, thinking some deep-knee bends might limber her up. Finally he storms out in a high dudgeon, pulled by two white horses, maintaining that Juliet must marry Paris or else. The alternative is too terrible to relate.

"Do as thou wilt," says Lady Capulet, washing her hands of the affair, and toweling briskly.

But does Juliet wilt? No. She has a lot of spunk, that girl. Things look black, but she will go to Friar Laurence. *He* will know what to do.

A desperate plan

It is now Tuesday, and time is short. If something isn't done by Thursday, Juliet will have two husbands and will be twice as nervous as the usual bride.

But the good Friar has a plan. It is long and intricate and he has obviously been working on it for days, when he should have been praying or gathering weeds.

"Take thou this vial," he tells Juliet. When she goes to bed Wednesday night, if she will swallow "the distilling liquor,"[24] it will make her stop breathing, turn cold, and look as good as dead. "The roses in thy

---

22. He doesn't specify high hurdle or low, but either would do.
23. Juliet still hasn't removed that cold cream.
24. The Friar does a little medicinal moonshining in back of the cloister.

lips and cheeks shall fade to paly ashes," he says, "and thy eyes' windows fall." He can see it vividly, even the little shutters in front of her eyes, and is in an ecstasy of ghoulish delight.

On Thursday morning, the Friar continues, Paris will come to her bedroom to rouse her and, thinking her deceased, change his mind about marriage. She will then be borne on a bier to the Capulet vault and left to become one of the family skeletons. After forty-two hours (so it says on the label), the effect of the medicine will wear off and Juliet will wake up without even a hangover. Meanwhile the Friar will have posted an epistle to Romeo, explaining the whole complicated business, and Romeo will be right there in the vault[25] when Juliet awakens, and can carry her off to Mantua.

It's a gruesome scheme, but Juliet is not to be outdone when it comes to thinking up macabre ideas.

"O, bid me leap from off the battlements, chain me with roaring bears, or shut me nightly in a charnelhouse," she beseeches the Friar. But he thinks his plan is preferable, having more confidence in poisons.

Juliet trudges homeward, clutching the vial in her hot little hand. Because of her youth, she is unaware that the traditional way to get rid of an unwelcome suitor is to give *him* the poison.

The denouement (how it comes out)

At first everything goes as planned. Juliet shakes well before using, takes a deep draught, and falls on the bed senseless, without even time to slip out of her street clothes. In the morning the Nurse tries to wake

25. Watch in hand, counting off the seconds.

her and discovers she is sleeping the Long Sleep.[26] Lamentation ensues.

"O day! O day!" cries the Nurse.

"O child! O child!" cries Capulet.

"O love! O life" cries Paris, with a little more variety.

The only good thing about the whole affair, as the Father of the Bride[27] observes, is the fact that the flowers ordered for the wedding will do very nicely for the funeral.

So Juliet, in her burying clothes, is stowed away in the family vault with Tybalt and sundry other decomposed kinfolk. Pale though she is, she's the best-looking thing in the place.

But now matters go awry. The friar whom Friar Laurence sent "with speed to Mantua" either was arrested for speeding or took a wrong turn. Anyhow, word fails to reach Romeo about Juliet's true condition. He hears that she is dead, and forthwith rushes out and buys some poison of his own. His idea is to imbibe it in the Capulet burial vault, so that at least he can have the pleasure of being dead in the same place with Juliet.

However, when he gets to the tomb and pries his way in with "an iron crow" (either a misprint for "crowbar" or a mighty tough bird), he finds Paris already there. Paris came not to die but to bring flowers, but Romeo changes all that with a few thrusts of his sword. Some of Shakespeare's best dialogue ensues.

ROMEO. Have at thee, boy. *[They fight.]*
PARIS. O, I am slain! *[Falls.]*

Thereupon he dies (also in square brackets), and

26. But athwart rather than lengthwise.
27. Henceforth referred to as the Father of the Corpse.

Romeo turns back to the business at hand. "Here will I remain," he remarks gloomily to the prettiest corpse, "with worms that are thy chamber-maids." The picture conjured up, of worms bustling about with little white caps on their heads, dusting the ledges, is one of Shakespeare's most masterful.

Then, sealing Juliet's lips with a kiss, to keep them watertight, he quaffs the poison and is dead even before he can make a long speech.[28]

Just after the nick of time, Friar Laurence arrives with a lantern, another of those iron crows, and a spade. At the same time (exactly forty-two hours, to the second) Juliet awakens refreshed. Seeing the bodies of Paris and Romeo, and figuring everything out at a glance, she snatches up Romeo's dagger.

"O happy dagger!" she says as she thrusts the lucky blade into her bosom. "This is thy sheath; there rust, and let me die." As soon as she can arrange her robe tastefully and fold her hands in the approved manner, she expires. The Friar might have saved her had he not been momentarily distracted by the arrival of the Watch, a large crowd of people who like to stare intently at anything gruesome.

Shortly the tomb is full of sightseers and well-wishers. In a moment of generosity, Montague promises to have a solid-gold statue of Juliet erected in the town square, thereby reminding American tourists of what put Verona on the map.

It's too bad about Romeo and Juliet, but anyhow Montague and Capulet bury the hatchet.[29] They exeunt arm in arm, hand in glove, and tongue in cheek.[30]

28. This is the only valid internal evidence that Shakespeare might not have written this play.
29. And not, as might have been anticipated earlier, in each other.
30. Legend has it that they went into business together, selling postcards and souvenirs.

Love

by Takasaki Masakaze,
translated by Miyamori Asataro

*In this poem Takasaki Masakaze, a 20th
century Japanese poet, presents a timeless
dilemma experienced by many teens,
including both Juliet and Romeo.*

Oh, never before have I known, among
    All my heart's sentiments,
One that was hard for me to confide
    To my own parents.

Invitation to Love

by Paul Laurence Dunbar

*Paul Laurence Dunbar was a popular poet
at the turn of the century. Juliet might
have expressed her feelings about her
husband with this poem.*

Come when the nights are bright with stars
    Or when the moon is mellow;
Come when the sun his golden bars
    Drops on the hay-field yellow.
5   Come in the twilight soft and gray,
Come in the night or come in the day,
Come, O Love, whene'er you may,
    And you are welcome, welcome.

You are sweet, O Love, dear Love,
10 You are soft as the nesting dove.
Come to my heart and bring it rest
As the bird flies home to its welcome nest.

Come when my heart is full of grief
    Or when my heart is merry;
15 Come with the falling of the leaf
    Or with the redd'ning cherry.
Come when the year's first blossom blows,
Come when the summer gleams and glows,
Come with the winter's drifting snows,
20   And you are welcome, welcome.

The Wooing of Ariadne

by Harry Mark Petrakis

In this story, a modern Romeo falls for an unwilling Juliet. As you read this romance about two Greek-Americans, think about other connections that link the story to Shakespeare's play.

I knew from the beginning she must accept my love—put aside foolish female protestations. It is the distinction of the male to be the aggressor and the cloak of the female to lend grace to the pursuit. Aha! I am wise to these wiles.

I first saw Ariadne at a dance given by the Spartan brotherhood in the Legion Hall on Laramie Street. The usual assemblage of prune-faced and banana-bodied women smelling of virtuous anemia. They were an outrage to a man such as myself.

Then I saw her! A tall stately woman, perhaps in her early thirties. She had firm and slender arms bare to the shoulders and a graceful neck. Her hair was black and thick and piled in a great bun at the back of her head. That grand abundance of hair attracted me at once. This modern aberration women have of chopping their hair close to the scalp and leaving it in fantastic disarray I find revolting.

I went at once to my friend Vasili, the baker, and asked him who she was.

"Ariadne Langos," he said. "Her father is Janco Langos, the grocer."

"Is she engaged or married?"

"No," he said slyly. "They say she frightens off the young men. They say she is very spirited."

"Excellent," I said and marveled at my good fortune in finding her unpledged. "Introduce me at once."

"Marko," Vasili said with some apprehension. "Do not commit anything rash."

I pushed the little man forward. "Do not worry, little friend," I said. "I am a man suddenly possessed by a vision. I must meet her at once."

We walked together across the dance floor to where my beloved stood. The closer we came the more impressive was the majestic swell of her breasts and the fine great sweep of her thighs. She towered over the insignificant apple-core women around her. Her eyes, dark and thoughtful, seemed to be restlessly searching the room.

Be patient, my dove! Marko is coming.

"Miss Ariadne," Vasili said. "This is Mr. Marko Palamas. He desires to have the honor of your acquaintance."

She looked at me for a long and piercing moment. I imagined her gauging my mighty strength by the width of my shoulders and the circumference of my arms. I felt the tips of my mustache bristle with pleasure. Finally she nodded with the barest minimum of courtesy. I was not discouraged.

"Miss Ariadne," I said, "may I have the pleasure of this dance?"

She stared at me again with her fiery eyes. I could imagine more timid men shriveling before her fierce gaze. My heart flamed at the passion her rigid exterior concealed.

"I think not," she said.

"Don't you dance?"

Vasili gasped beside me. An old prune-face standing nearby clucked her toothless gums.

"Yes, I dance," Ariadne said coolly. "I do not wish to dance with you."

"Why?" I asked courteously.

"I do not think you heard me," she said. "I do not wish to dance with you."

Oh, the sly and lovely darling. Her subterfuge so apparent. Trying to conceal her pleasure at my interest.

"Why?" I asked again.

"I am not sure," she said. "It could be your appearance, which bears considerable resemblance to a gorilla, or your manner, which would suggest closer alliance to a pig."

"Now that you have met my family," I said engagingly, "let us dance."

"Not now," she said, and her voice rose. "Not this dance or the one after. Not tonight or tomorrow night or next month or next year. Is that clear?"

Sweet, sweet Ariadne. Ancient and eternal game of retreat and pursuit. My pulse beat more quickly.

Vasili pulled at my sleeve. He was my friend, but without the courage of a goat. I shook him off and spoke to Ariadne.

"There is a joy like fire that consumes a man's heart when he first sets eyes on his beloved," I said. "This I felt when I first saw you." My voice trembled under a mighty passion. "I swear before God from this moment that I love you."

She stared shocked out of her deep dark eyes and, beside her, old prune-face staggered as if she had been kicked. Then my beloved did something which proved indisputably that her passion was as intense as mine.

She doubled up her fist and struck me in the eye. A stout blow for a woman that brought a haze to my vision, but I shook my head and moved a step closer.

"I would not care," I said, "if you struck out both my eyes. I would cherish the memory of your beauty forever."

By this time the music had stopped, and the dancers formed a circle of idiot faces about us. I paid them no attention and ignored Vasili, who kept whining and pulling at my sleeve.

"You are crazy!" she said. "You must be mad! Remove yourself from my presence or I will tear out both your eyes and your tongue besides!"

You see! Another woman would have cried, or been frightened into silence. But my Ariadne, worthy and venerable, hurled her spirit into my teeth.

"I would like to call on your father tomorrow," I said. From the assembled dancers who watched there rose a few vagrant whispers and some rude laughter. I stared at them carefully and they hushed at once. My temper and strength of arm were well known.

Ariadne did not speak again, but in a magnificent spirit stamped from the floor. The music began, and men and women began again to dance. I permitted Vasili to pull me to a corner.

"You are insane!" he said. He wrung his withered fingers in anguish. "You assaulted her like a Turk! Her relatives will cut out your heart!"

"My intentions were honorable," I said. "I saw her and loved her and told her so." At this point I struck my fist against my chest. Poor Vasili jumped.

"But you do not court a woman that way," he said.

"*You* don't, my anemic friend," I said. "Nor do the rest of these sheep. But I court a woman that way!"

He looked to heaven and helplessly shook his head. I waved good-by and started for my hat and coat.

"Where are you going?" he asked.

"To prepare for tomorrow," I said. "In the morning I will speak to her father."

I left the hall and in the street felt the night wind cold on my flushed cheeks. My blood was inflamed. The memory of her loveliness fed fuel to the fire. For the first time I understood with a terrible clarity the driven heroes of the past performing mighty deeds in love. Paris stealing Helen in passion, and Menelaus pursuing with a great fleet. In that moment if I knew the whole world would be plunged into conflict I would have followed Ariadne to Hades.

I went to my rooms above my tavern. I could not sleep. All night I tossed in restless frenzy. I touched my eye that she had struck with her spirited hand.

Ariadne! Ariadne! my soul cried out.

In the morning I bathed and dressed carefully. I confirmed the address of Langos, the grocer, and started to his store. It was a bright cold November morning, but I walked with spring in my step.

When I opened the door of the Langos grocery, a tiny bell rang shrilly. I stepped into the store piled with fruits and vegetables and smelling of cabbages and greens.

A stooped little old man with white bushy hair and owlish eyes came toward me. He looked as if his veins contained vegetable juice instead of blood, and if he were, in truth, the father of my beloved I marveled at how he could have produced such a paragon of women.

"Are you Mr. Langos?"

"I am," he said and he came closer. "I am."

"I met your daughter last night," I said. "Did she mention I was going to call?"

He shook his head somberly.

"My daughter mentioned you," he said. "In thirty years I have never seen her in such a state of agitation. She was possessed."

"The effect on me was the same," I said. "We met for the first time last night, and I fell passionately in love."

"Incredible," the old man said.

"You wish to know something about me," I said.

"My name is Marko Palamas. I am a Spartan emigrated to this country eleven years ago. I am forty-one years old. I have been a wrestler and a sailor and fought with the resistance movement in Greece in the war. For this service I was decorated by the king. I own a small but profitable tavern on Dart Street. I attend church regularly. I love your daughter."

As I finished he stepped back and bumped a rack of fruit. An orange rolled off to the floor. I bent and retrieved it to hand it to him, and he cringed as if he thought I might bounce it off his old head.

"She is a bad-tempered girl," he said. "Stubborn, impatient and spoiled. She has been the cause of considerable concern to me. All the eligible young men have been driven away by her temper and disposition."

"Poor girl," I said. "Subjected to the courting of calves and goats."

The old man blinked his owlish eyes. The front door opened and a battleship of a woman sailed in.

"Three pounds of tomatoes, Mr. Langos," she said. "I am in a hurry. Please to give me good ones. Last week two spoiled before I had a chance to put them into Demetri's salad."

"I am very sorry," Mr. Langos said. He turned to me. "Excuse me, Mr. Poulmas."

"Palamas," I said. "Marko Palamas."

He nodded nervously. He went to wait on the battleship, and I spent a moment examining the store. Neat and small. I would not imagine he did more than hold his own. In the rear of the store there were stairs leading to what appeared to be an apartment above. My heart beat faster.

When he had bagged the tomatoes and given change, he returned to me and said, "She is also a terrible cook. She cannot fry an egg without burning it." His voice shook with woe. "She cannot make pilaf or lamb with squash." He paused. "You like pilaf and lamb with squash?"

"Certainly."

"You see?" he said in triumph. "She is useless in the kitchen. She is thirty years old, and I am resigned she will remain an old maid. In a way I am glad because I know she would drive some poor man to drink."

"Do not deride her to discourage me," I said. "You need have no fear that I will mistreat her or cause her unhappiness. When she is married to me she will cease being a problem to you." I paused. "It is true that I am not pretty by the foppish standards that prevail today. But I am a man. I wrestled Zahundos and pinned him two straight falls in Baltimore. A giant of a man. Afterward he conceded he had met his master. This from Zahundos was a mighty compliment."

"I am sure," the old man said without enthusiasm. "I am sure."

He looked toward the front door as if hoping for another customer.

"Is your daughter upstairs?"

He looked startled and tugged at his apron. "Yes," he said. "I don't know. Maybe she has gone out."

"May I speak to her? Would you kindly tell her I wish to speak with her."

"You are making a mistake," the old man said. "A terrible mistake."

"No mistake," I said firmly.

The old man shuffled toward the stairs. He climbed them slowly. At the top he paused and turned the knob of the door. He rattled it again.

"It is locked," he called down. "It has never been locked before. She has locked the door."

"Knock," I said. "Knock to let her know I am here."

"I think she knows," the old man said. "I think she knows."

He knocked gently.

"Knock harder," I suggested. "Perhaps she does not hear."

"I think she hears," the old man said. "I think she hears."

"Knock again," I said. "Shall I come up and knock for you?"

"No, no," the old man said quickly. He gave the door a sound kick. Then he groaned as if he might have hurt his foot.

"She does not answer," he said in a quavering voice. "I am very sorry she does not answer."

"The coy darling," I said and laughed. "If that is her game." I started for the front door of the store.

I went out and stood on the sidewalk before the store. Above the grocery were the front windows of their apartment. I cupped my hands about my mouth.

"Ariadne!" I shouted. "Ariadne!"

The old man came out the door running disjointedly. He looked frantically down the street.

"Are you mad?" he asked shrilly. "You will cause a riot. The police will come. You must be mad!"

"Ariadne!" I shouted. "Beloved!"

A window slammed open, and the face of Ariadne appeared above me. Her dark hair tumbled about her ears.

"Go away!" she shrieked. "Will you go away!"

"Ariadne," I said loudly. "I have come as I promised. I have spoken to your father. I wish to call on you."

"Go away!" she shrieked. "Madman! Imbecile! Go away!"

By this time a small group of people had assembled around the store and were watching curiously. The old man stood wringing his hands and uttering what sounded like small groans.

"Ariadne," I said. "I wish to call on you. Stop this nonsense and let me in."

She pushed farther out the window and showed me her teeth.

"Be careful, beloved," I said. "You might fall."

She drew her head in quickly, and I turned then to the assembled crowd.

"A misunderstanding," I said. "Please move on."

Suddenly old Mr. Langos shrieked. A moment later something broke on the sidewalk a foot from where I stood. A vase or a plate. I looked up, and Ariadne was preparing to hurl what appeared to be a water pitcher.

"Ariadne!" I shouted. "Stop that!"

The water pitcher landed closer than the vase, and fragments of glass struck my shoes. The crowd scattered, and the old man raised his hands and wailed to heaven.

Ariadne slammed down the window.

The crowd moved in again a little closer, and somewhere among them I heard laughter. I fixed them with a cold stare and waited for some one of them to say something offensive. I would have tossed him around like sardines, but they slowly dispersed and moved on. In another moment the old man and I were alone.

I followed him into the store. He walked an awkward dance of agitation. He shut the door and peered out through the glass.

"A disgrace," he wailed. "A disgrace. The whole street will know by nightfall. A disgrace."

"A girl of heroic spirit," I said. "Will you speak to her for me? Assure her of the sincerity of my feelings. Tell her I pledge eternal love and devotion."

The old man sat down on an orange crate and weakly made his cross.

"I had hoped to see her myself," I said. "But if you promise to speak to her, I will return this evening."

"That soon?" the old man said.

"If I stayed now," I said, "it would be sooner."

"This evening," the old man said and shook his head in resignation. "This evening."

I went to my tavern for a while and set up the glasses for the evening trade. I made arrangements for Pavlakis to tend bar in my place. Afterward I sat alone in my apartment and read a little of majestic Pindar to ease the agitation of my heart.

Once in the mountains of Greece when I fought with the guerrillas in the last year of the great war, I suffered a wound from which it seemed I would die. For days high fever raged in my body. My friends brought a priest at night secretly from one of the captive villages to read the last rites. I accepted the coming of death and was grateful for many things. For the gentleness and wisdom of my old grandfather, the loyalty of my companions in war, the years I sailed between the wild ports of the seven seas, and the strength that flowed to me from the Spartan earth. For one thing only did I weep when it seemed I would leave life, that I had never set ablaze the world with a burning song of passion for one woman. Women I had known, pockets of pleasure that I tumbled for quick joy, but I had been denied mighty love for one woman. For that I wept.

In Ariadne I swore before God I had found my woman. I knew by the storm-lashed hurricane that swept within my body. A woman whose majesty was in harmony with the earth, who would be faithful and beloved to me as Penelope had been to Ulysses.

That evening near seven I returned to the grocery. Deep twilight had fallen across the street, and the lights in the window of the store had been dimmed. The apples and oranges and pears had been covered with brown paper for the night.

I tried the door and found it locked. I knocked on the glass, and a moment later the old man came shuffling out of the shadows and let me in.

"Good evening, Mr. Langos."

He muttered some greeting in answer. "Ariadne is not here," he said. "She is at the church. Father Marlas wishes to speak with you."

"A fine young priest," I said. "Let us go at once."

I waited on the sidewalk while the old man locked the store. We started the short walk to the church.

"A clear and ringing night," I said. "Does it not make you feel the wonder and glory of being alive?"

The old man uttered what sounded like a groan, but a truck passed on the street at that moment and I could not be sure.

At the church we entered by a side door leading to the office of Father Marlas. I knocked on the door, and when he called to us to enter we walked in.

Young Father Marlas was sitting at his desk in his black cassock and with his black goatee trim and imposing beneath his clean-shaven cheeks. Beside the desk, in a dark blue dress sat Ariadne, looking somber and beautiful. A bald-headed, big-nosed old man with flint and fire in his eyes sat in a chair beside her.

"Good evening, Marko," Father Marlas said and smiled.

"Good evening, Father," I said.

"Mr. Langos and his daughter you have met," he said and he cleared his throat. "This is Uncle Paul Langos."

"Good evening, Uncle Paul," I said. He glared at me and did not answer. I smiled warmly at Ariadne in greeting, but she was watching the priest.

"Sit down," Father Marlas said.

I sat down across from Ariadne, and old Mr. Langos took a chair beside Uncle Paul. In this way we were arrayed in battle order as if we were opposing armies.

A long silence prevailed during which Father Marlas cleared his throat several times. I observed Ariadne closely. There were grace and poise even in the way her slim-fingered hands rested in her lap. She was a dark and lovely flower, and my pulse beat more quickly at her nearness.

"Marko," Father Marlas said finally. "Marko, I have known you well for the three years since I assumed duties in this parish. You are most regular in your devotions and very generous at the time of the Christmas and Easter offerings. Therefore, I find it hard to believe this complaint against you."

"My family are not liars!" Uncle Paul said, and he had a voice like hunks of dry hard cheese being grated.

"Of course not," Father Marlas said quickly. He smiled benevolently at Ariadne. "I only mean to say—"

"Tell him to stay away from my niece," Uncle Paul burst out.

"Excuse me, Uncle Paul," I said very politely. "Will you kindly keep out of what is not your business."

Uncle Paul looked shocked. "Not my business?" He looked from Ariadne to Father Marlas and then to his brother. "Not my business?"

"This matter concerns Ariadne and me," I said. "With outside interference it becomes more difficult."

"Not my business!" Uncle Paul said. He couldn't seem to get that through his head.

"Marko," Father Marlas said, and his composure was slightly shaken. "The family feels you are forcing your attention upon this girl. They are concerned."

"I understand, Father," I said. "It is natural for them to be concerned. I respect their concern. It is also natural for me to speak of love to a woman I have chosen for my wife."

"Not my business!" Uncle Paul said again, and shook his head violently.

"My daughter does not wish to become your wife," Mr. Langos said in a squeaky voice.

"That is for your daughter to say," I said courteously.

Ariadne made a sound in her throat, and we all looked at her. Her eyes were deep and cold, and she spoke slowly and carefully as if weighing each word on a scale in her father's grocery.

"I would not marry this madman if he were one of the Twelve Apostles," she said.

"See!" Mr. Langos said in triumph.

"Not my business!" Uncle Paul snarled.

"Marko," Father Marlas said. "Try to understand."

"We will call the police!" Uncle Paul raised his voice. "Put this hoodlum under a bond!"

"Please!" Father Marlas said. "Please!"

"Today he stood on the street outside the store," Mr. Langos said excitedly. "He made me a laughingstock."

"If I were a younger man," Uncle Paul growled, "I would settle this without the police. Zi-ip!" He drew a callused finger violently across his throat.

"Please," Father Marlas said.

"A disgrace!" Mr. Langos said.

"An outrage!" Uncle Paul said.

"He must leave Ariadne alone!" Mr. Langos said.

"We will call the police!" Uncle Paul said.

"Silence!" Father Marlas said loudly.

With everything suddenly quiet he turned to me. His tone softened.

"Marko," he said and he seemed to be pleading a little. "Marko, you must understand."

Suddenly a great bitterness assailed me, and anger at myself, and a terrible sadness that flowed like night through my body because I could not make them understand.

"Father," I said quietly, "I am not a fool. I am Marko Palamas and once I pinned the mighty Zahundos in Baltimore. But this battle, more important to me by far, I have lost. That which has not the grace of God is better far in silence."

I turned to leave and it would have ended there.

"Hoodlum!" Uncle Paul said. "It is time you were silent!"

I swear in that moment if he had been a younger man I would have flung him to the dome of the church. Instead I turned and spoke to them all in fire and fury.

"Listen," I said. "I feel no shame for the violence of my feelings. I am a man bred of the Spartan earth and my emotions are violent. Let those who squeak of life feel shame. Nor do I feel shame because I saw this flower and loved her. Or because I spoke at once of my love."

No one moved or made a sound.

"We live in a dark age," I said. "An age where men say one thing and mean another. A time of dwarfs afraid of life. The days are gone when mighty Pindar sang his radiant blossoms of song. When the noble passions of men set ablaze cities, and the heroic deeds of men rang like thunder to every corner of the earth."

I spoke my final words to Ariadne. "I saw you and loved you," I said gently. "I told you of my love. This is my way—the only way I know. If this way has proved offensive to you I apologize to you alone. But understand clearly that for none of this do I feel shame."

I turned then and started to the door. I felt my heart weeping as if waves were breaking within my body.

"Marko Palamas," Ariadne said. I turned slowly. I looked at her. For the first time the warmth I was sure dwelt in her body radiated within the circles of her face. For the first time she did not look at me with her eyes like glaciers.

"Marko Palamas," she said and there was a strange moving softness in the way she spoke my name. "You may call on me tomorrow."

Uncle Paul shot out of his chair. "She is mad too!" he shouted. "He has bewitched her!"

"A disgrace!" Mr. Langos said.

"Call the police!" Uncle Paul shouted. "I'll show him if it's my business!"

"My poor daughter!" Mr. Langos wailed.

"Turk!" Uncle Paul shouted. "Robber!"

"Please!" Father Marlas said. "Please!"

I ignored them all. In that winged and zestful moment I had eyes only for my beloved, for Ariadne, blossom of my heart and black-eyed flower of my soul!

from A Natural History of Love

by Diane Ackerman

In Romeo's day there were some unstated rules to follow about courting. In this essay, author Diane Ackerman explains the rules of love in the 16th century.

Arranged marriages were a hand-me-down custom known to all, but at about this time, amazingly, a significant number of people began to object. Shakespeare's plays are filled with collisions over the right to choose whom to marry, and complaints by couples who'd prefer a love match. Shakespeare didn't invent the best known of them, Romeo and Juliet, leading characters in a classic that had been told in sundry cultures and genres. In the second century A.D., Xenophon of Ephesus presented the story as *Anthia and Abrocomas,* but it may have been older than that. Over the years it fed many imaginations, and its hero and heroine changed names. In 1535, Luigi da Porto spun the tale as a slow-moving melodrama in a novel with an eighteen-year-old heroine named *La Giuletta.* The story was still being written in the latter half of the sixteenth century, in poetry and prose, and even the distinguished Spanish writer Lope de Vega wrote a drama called *Capulets and Montagues.* In telling the story yet again, Shakespeare was doing what Leonard Bernstein and collaborators did with *West Side Story,* putting a well-known, shopworn tale into contemporary dress, locale, and issues. They knew people would identify with the heartbreak of "Juliet and her

Romeo,"* as it's so often described, focusing on the romantic hopes of the girl. Referring to it in that way makes "Romeo" sound less like a man than a condition or trait possessed by Juliet.

A beautiful, chaste Veronese girl, whose very name is rhyme (Juliet Capulet) encounters a boy who embodies her robust sensuality. He is passion incarnate, someone in love with love. "Love is a smoke made with the fume of sighs," he at first tells his friend Benvolio, and then decides it isn't gentle, but "too rough, / Too rude, too boisterous, and it pricks like thorn." On the rebound from a girl named Rosaline, and electric with need, Romeo is like lightning looking for a place to strike. He meets Juliet and the play's thunderstorm of emotions begins.

The story hinges on the rivalry between two noble houses, and the forbidden love of their children, Romeo and Juliet. Chance, destiny, and good playwriting ordain that they shall meet and become "star-crossed lovers" with a sad, luminous fate. Typically adolescent, the lovers feel the same bliss, suffer the same torments, and tackle the same obstacles young lovers always have. One age-old note is that they must keep their love a secret from their parents, a theme beautifully expressed in the ancient Egyptian love poems. The erotic appeal of the forbidden stranger also is an old theme, whether he's from the enemy's camp or just "the wrong side of the tracks." So is the notion of love as detachment, a force that pulls you away from your family, your past, your friends, even your neighborhood. Old, too, is the idea of love as a madness; and the fetishistic desire to be an

*The closing lines of the play are:

> For never was a story of more woe
> Than this of Juliet and her Romeo.

article of clothing worn by the beloved ("O, that I were a glove upon that hand, / That I might touch that cheek!" Romeo cries), echoing, centuries later, the Egyptian love poet's desire to "be her ring, the seal on her finger."

Shakespeare made important changes in his telling of the story. In his play, Juliet is thirteen years old; in the other versions she's older. In his play, she and Romeo only know one another for four days in July; in other versions, the courtship lasts months. Even if we accept the gossip of his time that Italian girls mature faster than English ones—why does he make the couple so young and their love instantaneous? Shakespeare was about thirty when he wrote the play, and as his exquisite sonnets declare, he knew love's terrain. Indeed, in one sonnet he laments the mistake of introducing his male lover to his female lover. Apparently, they fell for each other and left Shakespeare high and dry, in double grief. I think he wished to demonstrate in *Romeo and Juliet* how reckless, labile, and ephemeral the emotion of love is, especially in young people, and especially if one compares it with the considered love of older people. Most of the heroines in his other plays are also very young.* Throughout the plays, one finds the tenets of courtly love, but with two exceptions: love always leads to matrimony, and Shakespeare does not condone adultery. The lovers have to be young, of good social rank, well dressed, and of virtuous character. The man has to be courageous, the woman chaste and beautiful. Rarely are the lovers introduced. They fall in love at first sight, the beauty of the beloved's face signaling everything they need to know.

*For example, both Miranda in *The Tempest* and Viola in *Twelfth Night* are only about fifteen, and Marina in *Pericles* is fourteen.

Danger usually lurks close by, but they are headstrong, powerless to resist love. The lovers are constantly obsessed with each other. They credit the object of their affection with godlike qualities, and go through religious rituals of worship and devotion. They exchange talismans—a ring, a scarf, or some meaningful trifle. A medieval lady gave her knight a piece of clothing or jewelry to protect him, a kind of love charm. Lovers still exchange such tokens today, and imbue them with similar power. During the Middle Ages, lovers were secretive, often so that the woman's husband wouldn't discover her infidelity. In Elizabethan times, lovers were still secretive, but then it was to keep the girl's father from preventing their meetings. When Shakespeare's lovers declare their love, they intend to marry. An ordeal keeps them temporarily apart, and during this lonely, dislocated time, they weep and sigh, become forgetful, lose their appetites, moan to their confidants, write elegant, heartfelt love letters, lie awake all night. The play ends with marriage and/or death. These are the only choices open to Shakespearean lovers, because they can only love one person, without whom life seems worthless. In Shakespeare's plays, the characters all practice courtly love, but there is one important difference: instead of craving seduction, they crave marriage. Their families might be mad as hell, go to war over it, or send the girl off to a nunnery. But the lovers don't need their parents' legal permission to marry. When love conquers all, it isn't through subterfuge or blackmail or because of pregnancy, but because the parents understand the sincerity of the couple's love.

As *Romeo and Juliet* unfolds, the main characters make it clear that there are many forms of love. T.J.B. Spencer sums this up in his commentary to the Penguin edition:

There is Juliet's—both before and after she has fallen in love; Romeo's—both while he thinks he is in love with Rosaline, and after his passion has been truly aroused by Juliet; Mercutio's—his brilliant intelligence seems to make ridiculous an all-absorbing and exclusive passion based upon sex; Friar Laurence's—for him love is an accompaniment of life, reprehensible if violent or unsanctified by religion; Father Capulet's—for him it is something to be decided by a prudent father for his heiress-daughter; Lady Capulet's—for her it is a matter of worldly wisdom (she herself is not yet thirty and has a husband who gave up dancing thirty years ago); and the Nurse's—for her, love is something natural and sometimes lasting, connected with pleasure and pregnancy, part of the round of interests in a woman's life.

The teenagers of *Romeo and Juliet* are hotheads, or hot loins, who decide that they are mortally in love and must marry immediately, though they haven't exchanged a hundred words. "Give me my Romeo," Juliet demands, with an innocence blunt and trusting. But even she fears the speed at which they're moving:

> It is too rash, too unadvised, too sudden;
> Too like the lightning, which doth cease to be
> Ere one can say it lightens.

The use of lightning and gunpowder images throughout the play keeps reminding us how combustible the situation is, how incandescent their love, and how life itself burns like a brief, gorgeous spark in the night. Their moonlit balcony scene, full of tenderness and yearning, with some of the most beautiful phrasing ever written, shows them sighing for love under the moon and stars, vibrantly alive in a world of glitter and shadow. After such intimacy under the covers of night, their secret marriage is certain. Then comes the impossibility of living without one another. After many obstacles, a set of dire confusions leads the lovers to commit suicide. Ironically, the horror of their deaths serves to reconcile the feuding families. Thus love is portrayed as an emissary force that can travel between foes and conduct its own arbitration. On the most basic level, this is biologically true, however one expresses it, as *competing organisms join forces for mutual benefit*, or *love can make bedfellows of enemies*. Why does the world seem unlivable without the loved one? Why does a teenager abandon hope of ever loving or being loved again in the entirety of his or her life?

Romeo and Juliet in Sarajevo

by John Zaritsky

Stories of forbidden love do not only appear in fictional plays. Recently, journalists for the PBS television program Frontline *told the real life drama of Admira Ismic and Bosko Brkic, two young people from the former Yugoslavia. The following is a transcript of the broadcast that aired in May 1994.*

Zijo Ismic. *[through interpreter]* I still don't believe that they're dead because it's very hard to believe such young people like that can disappear with such a sudden and violent death. All their wishes, all their plans are sunk after one bullet, after one burst, after one move, after one monstrous act.

Announcer. Tonight on *Frontline,* love and death in Sarajevo. She was a Muslim, he was a Serb. As a young couple, they tried to build a future, defying the hatred that was tearing their country apart. But a year ago, trying to escape, they were struck by sniper's bullets and died in each other's arms. Tonight on *Frontline,* "Romeo and Juliet in Sarajevo."

Narrator. For two years, the world watched while Sarajevo died—the shelling of the besieged city, the slaughter of the innocent civilians, the unending scenes of carnage and grief, overwhelming, numbing.

Dan Rather, CBS News. This is the CBS Evening News.

Narrator. But there was one picture and one story that seemed for a moment to break through the fatigue of horror.

1st Television Reporter. Here are some of this week's events around the world.

Narrator. A boy and a girl, one Serb, the other Muslim—

2nd Television Reporter. The war in Bosnia-Herzegovina has created—

Narrator. —dead in one another's arms on a bridge in no-man's land. They were called "the Romeo and Juliet of Sarajevo."

3rd Television Reporter. They died in each other's arms.

Narrator. This is their story.

Dan Rather. Two of the dead are a modern-day Romeo and Juliet, shot and killed by snipers in Sarajevo.

Narrator. Once upon a time, when they were 16, Bosko Brkic and Admira Ismic kissed at a New Year's Eve party. It was the beginning of 1984. That year, a Muslim girl and a Serbian boy fell in love for the first time in their lives. Admira's best friend in high school, Tanja Bogdanovic, knew them both well.

Tanja Bogdanovic. *[through interpreter]* The two of them were very, very different. I loved Admira because she was so different from me. She was very unusual. She was interested in things that were a little bit strange for a girl. She loved to drive motorcycles and she knew how to fix cars very well. She was a little bit of a wild character. Usually, girls are afraid of something, but nothing could scare Admira. Bosko was different. He was quieter and cooler. He had a smile all the time. He liked to play jokes on people, but in a nice way, like a real nice guy. He had a real charm that you don't see in people very often.

Narrator. Nineteen eighty-four was a magical time to be in Sarajevo. The city was hosting the winter Olympic games and Bosko and Admira saw the world come to their home. Historically, Sarajevo, the capital of Bosnia-Herzegovina, had always been a crossroads of nations, a city that had tried to set aside the old hatreds, the embodiment of an international dream. It was a cosmopolitan place, a melting pot where Muslims, Serbs, Croats, Jews and other nationalities had lived together for more than 500 years.

Bosko's parents came here from Serbia in 1970. Dragen was an engineer who worked for the United Nations. Rada was a chemist. They had two sons, Bosko and Bane.

Rada Brkic. *[through interpreter]* I raised them without thinking about religion or nationality. I never said, "You are Serbs, they are Muslims or Croats." I didn't regard her as a Muslim, as different. I saw her only as the girlfriend of my son, who loved her, and who I loved, too.

Narrator. Admira's Muslim parents were just as welcoming to Bosko. Zijo Ismic, a prosperous garage owner, and his wife, Nera, approved of their eldest daughter's first serious boyfriend.

Zijo Ismic. *[through interpreter]* Well, I knew from the first day about that relationship and I didn't have anything against it. I thought it was good because the guy was so likable. And after a time, I started to love him and didn't regard him any differently than

Admira.

Nera Ismic. *[through interpreter]* In my family, there are many mixed marriages. Two aunts of mine are married to Serbs. They have kids who are my relatives, so that means I can't see a difference. And we lived like that the entire time before the war. All of us—or should I say most of us only judge people as people, not which nationality they are. But people who think differently made this war. We didn't care about nationalities. That wasn't important to us.

Mr. Ismic. *[through interpreter]* My best friend, Otto, is a Croat. I spent more time in his Catholic church than in all the mosques of the world. Besides, I've never been in a mosque, but I went to church with him because his parents were religious and they were going to church. I was Otto's friend, and wherever he went, I went. I even sang in the church choir and I didn't care. And that's something the world can't understand, is how a Muslim would sing in a church choir.

Narrator. For Admira's younger sister, Amela, that Bosko was a Serb and a Christian was not important. He was just the brother she'd never had.

Amela Ismic. *[through interpreter]* Bosko treated me like a younger sister. He always protected me and told me that if I ever had any problems, I could talk to him. "If somebody bothers you," he said, "tell me." He was like my brother.

Narrator. But Amela couldn't understand that, for her 80-year-old grandmother, accepting a mixed relationship wasn't so easy.

Sadika Ismic. *[through interpreter]* Yes. Yes, I did have something against it. I thought he is a Serb and she is a Muslim and how will it work? You know, some mixed marriages didn't last for a very long time—you know, some of them. You know how old people like me are thinking.

Narrator. What she was thinking about was her family's history, how her husband and brothers had fought the Serbs as part of a multi-ethnic force called "the Partisans" in the Second World War. They were fighting not just the Germans, but also Serbian nationalists known as Chetniks. The war had inflamed all the old nationalism. In neighboring Croatia, pro-Hitler fascists were rounding up Serbs in Nazi-like extermination programs. Bosko's grandmother remembers those times. She and her husband and her daughter, Rada, were living in a Serbian village in Croatia. One day, her husband was summoned to a police station.

Naka Gruber. *[through interpreter]* And then I never saw him again. I don't know where they took him. I just know he was killed. They said he was thrown in that Jadova pit near Gospic.

Narrator. Bosko's grandfather was one of an estimated 500,000 Serbs killed by the Croatian fascists. When the Partisan leader, Marshall Tito, emerged victorious at the end of the war, he had to contend with this legacy of deadly hatreds. His solution was to outlaw all expressions of nationalism. Everyone would now be a Yugoslav. A multi-ethnic youth corps, the Tito Pioneers, set out to rebuild the country. For Admira's father, Zijo, it was a time for hope.

Mr. Ismic. *[through interpreter]* I was a Tito Pioneer and I still believe in one idea. Tito was probably a visionary, and even now, I remember his words. "Keep brotherhood and unity in your eye." If we had succeeded in keeping to that, this war would not have happened.

Narrator. For the generation that followed, Yugoslavia became the most open society in Eastern Europe, with the freedom to travel and a standard of living closest to the West. When they graduated from high school in June, 1986, Bosko and Admira were typical Yugoslav teenagers. His mother says they were interested in cars, movies and music. But that summer, Bosko's father suddenly died from a heart attack. He was just 45. It was hard on Bosko. Three weeks later, he had to report for compulsory military duty in what was then the Yugoslav Federal Army. He was sent to an officer training school in Serbia.

Mr. Ismic. *[through interpreter]* Admira was very upset at the time he was in the army. You could see in her face that she loved Bosko. One day, I tried to help her, to say to her, "Go out. Go out with your friends. There are more guys than Bosko." That was my personal opinion. I thought the kid should go out and have a good time. But I could never convince her.

Mrs. Brkic. *[through interpreter]* Admira was really his first love. I can honestly say it was true love between them.

Narrator. They had never been apart before. He was 300 miles away. They wrote to each other almost every day.

1st Reader. "My dearest Admira: Every night when I go to bed, I cannot sleep because I'm thinking of you. My love, you are the only happiness I have."

2nd Reader. "My dear love: Sarajevo at night is the most beautiful thing in the world. I guess I could live somewhere else, but only if I must or if I'm forced. Just a little beat of time is left until we are together. After that, absolutely nothing can separate us."

1st Reader. "My dearest Admira: Truly, I miss you so much that I cannot say or explain in words. Now all my life points to the day when I'll finish my military service and see you again."

Narrator. After 11 months they were back together again. While Admira continued studying economics at university, Bosko set up a small kitchen-ware store stocked with products they'd buy on trips to Italy.

Meanwhile, across Eastern Europe communism was crumbling. But in Yugoslavia, an old force was reasserting itself. On an ancient battleground called "the Field of the Blackbirds," half a million Serbs gathered to honor their 14th century war hero, Prince Lazar. He had fought the Muslim Turks at the battle of Kosovo in 1389 and his defeat had not been forgotten. Now a militant Serbian politician, Slobodan Milosevic, used the threat of ancient enemies to stoke a rising Serbian nationalism with a call to re-claim their ancient territory.

Slobodan Milosevic. *[subtitles]* It is a coincidence of life and history that Serbia in 1989 is regaining its state and dignity. So in this way, we are celebrating a historic anniversary from the ancient past that has symbolic importance for the future of Serbia.

Narrator. In Croatia, the Serbian threat led to a declaration of independence in 1991. War broke out as Croatian forces battled the Serb-dominated Federal Army. History seemed to repeat itself. The old hatreds reasserted themselves as forces from both sides massacred civilians. Once again, Serbs in Croatia were forced to flee. Among them, after her house was destroyed for the second time in her life, Bosko's grandmother, Naka Gruber. Leaving literally everything behind, she finally joined relatives in Canada.

Mrs. Gruber. *[through interpreter]* Everything was looted and robbed, burned down. How couldn't it be hard? I see that there's no good fortune in anything. Since I was left without a husband, without a home, without anything, how can I be hopeful? How can I be happy?

Narrator. In the Serbian Orthodox church, she lit candles for the dead and prayed for the living, especially for her daughter and grandsons back in Bosnia, where people were still convinced that the war would not come to them.

Mrs. Gruber. *[through interpreter]* I told my daughter, Rada, before I came here, "Get out of Sarajevo. Take the kids and go to Serbia." I saw the situation was boiling over and would lead to great evil. And it was.

Narrator. On April 5th, 1992, the streets of Sarajevo were filled with Bosnian Muslims, Serbs and Croats demonstrating their support for a new, independent, multi-ethnic state. Sarajevans marched in the hope that they could hold on to their tradition of tolerance and avoid the bloodshed that followed Croatian independence. Suddenly, shots rang out. Bosnian Serbs loyal to a political party opposed to independence had fired into the crowd. A sniper's bullet claimed the first casualty of the Bosnian war. The siege of Sarajevo was about to begin.

Mr. Ismic. *[through interpreter]* I think that Bosko and Admira thought that everything would end soon. Even I thought that it would be 15 days, maybe a couple or three months, maximum. But it took time. Horrible things are going on and it's very hard to watch and live with that. But it's more horrible when you're a part of it. They felt very bad.

Narrator. There were, of course, many Serbs who

immediately left the city to join the Serbian army, people who had known Admira's father, Zijo, people like Father Voyislav Charkich, an orthodox priest.

Father Voyislav Charkich. *[through interpreter]* I went into the war voluntarily, as a priest and as a man, because the Orthodox church and the Serbian nation were in jeopardy. If we did not enter this war, within 10 years we would no longer be living on these lands. Even though the oldest object in the former Bosnia-Herzegovina is the old church in Sarajevo, which dates back to the 10th or 11th century.

Narrator. In a ceremony going back centuries, to the holy wars against the Muslims, Father Charkich blessed the elite Serbian soldiers, qualifying them to be known as Chetnik dukes.

Father Charkich. *[through interpreter]* We should all live with our own people. It's better for us to separate now, following this bloody war, so that my grandsons won't have to pick up a rifle, like I did. This is the last opportunity for accounts to be settled.

Narrator. On the other side, some Serbs stayed and joined the hastily assembled Bosnian defense forces, now dominated by Muslims. Bosko faced a hard decision.

Mrs. Brkic. *[through interpreter]* Bosko said, "I cannot go and shoot Serbs. I can't go into the Muslim army. If they call me, I simply cannot." He was talking once with one of his friends and said, "I simply cannot go and shoot Serbs" and he would not do that. Never. I know that for sure. But to go up into the hills and shoot back into Sarajevo—he couldn't do that, either, because Admira was there. Her parents were there and he couldn't do that, either. He was simply a kid who was not for the war.

Mr. Ismic. [through interpreter] Bosko stayed in Sarajevo because of his opinions of the war. He thought the same as I think. If he left Sarajevo, he'd never come back to his friends. He would be ashamed to face his buddies because if he left them, he would be a traitor.

Narrator. Misa Cuk, Bosko's Serbian neighbor, faced the same dilemma. Misa had sent his Muslim wife and children out of Sarajevo, but had stayed behind and joined the Bosnian army, to protect the city. With feelings against all Serbs running high, Misa was worried that if Bosko didn't fight, too, he might be killed by local gangs of Muslim extremists.

Misa Cuk. [through interpreter] I said, "Take this gun, because if somebody comes for you and it's time to die, at least you can protect yourself." He didn't want to take the gun. He didn't even want to hold it. He picked it up with two fingers, like his handkerchief.

Narrator. But every day on the streets of Sarajevo there was even greater danger. Anyone anywhere could suddenly become the target for a sniper's bullet. Every few hours a Serbian marksman would collect a bounty of 500 German marks reportedly placed on the head of every Sarajevan. It was a war where the hunter and his prey were often former friends and neighbors.

Mr. Ismic. [through interpreter] So many friends have gone over to the other side. That emptiness I'll never fill for the rest of my life. Those are friends I've spent a long time with, a good part of my life. Until yesterday, we were together, sitting together and drinking and celebrating together—Ramadans, Christmases, Orthodox Easters, Catholic Easters, birthdays, 29th of Novembers, Liberation Days and all of that. We celebrated together. What changed overnight? Who led the way for these people? Who had the power to lead the people, to take them from friends and bring them into the woods to shoot at us? I could never understand that.

Narrator. Every day Serbian artillery shells rained down on the city, killing and maiming even more innocent victims. Despite the terrifying risk, Bosko and Admira continued to see each other. Every day, one of them would walk across the city, traveling the five miles between the homes of their parents.

Mrs. Ismic. *[through interpreter]* I remember she told me once a shell landed near the bakery and some people died. That happened just after she crossed near the bakery. She couldn't stand the blood. She hid herself. She was horrified.

Mr. Ismic. *[through interpreter]* And they saw each other in a hail of bullets and a rain of shells. It didn't matter where in town—at Gram's place, here. Both of them, when they left their homes, faced the same risks, and Bosko and Admira were in the same danger.

Mrs. Brkic. *[through interpreter]* They fought some-times, like everybody else, but there wasn't a day when they didn't hear from each other. They always knew, for every moment, where each other was. I was sitting once with her alone and I asked her, "Can this war separate you from Bosko?" And she said, "Dear Rada, only bullets can."

Narrator. By July, 1992, Sarajevo was slowly being leveled. The Serb shells landed indiscriminately all over the city. Everyone—Croats, Muslims and Serbs—was vulnerable.

Mrs. Brkic. *[through interpreter]* We were in the living room, watching tennis, and just before, Bosko and a younger friend were in the kitchen. They left the kitchen just two minutes before the shell hit the

Romeo and Juliet in Sarajevo 289

apartment. He could have been killed there because shrapnel was everywhere.

Narrator. The random shell caused so much damage that Bosko and his mother had to abandon the apartment on Koshevo Hill, where they had lived for 25 years. They moved to another building next door, but just two weeks later another shell completely destroyed their new home. No one was hurt, but Rada decided she must now leave the neighborhood she loved.

Mrs. Brkic. *[through interpreter]* I left Koshevo Hill because of the constant shelling and it was very hard to go into shelters all the time. I was shaking every night. And Bosko was telling me all the time, "Mom, please go. Just you go. When you're safe, it will be easier for me to take care of myself. Now I'm worried, when you go out into the street, whether you will come back again or not."

Narrator. Admira's parents lived on a large property on the outskirts of the town. Zijo insisted that Rada should come and stay with them.

Mrs. Brkic. *[through interpreter]* I said to him once, "Zijo, maybe we'll have some problems with your neighbors because of me," and he said, "Nobody has the right to tell me what I can do in my own house or who should be in my house."

Mr. Ismic. *[through interpreter]* And the doors of my house and home are always open for her, so nobody pushed Rada to leave. She could have stayed. When she came over here, we didn't have any idea how long she would stay. All of us thought the war would soon be over. We didn't even think that she would go.

Mrs. Ismic. *[through interpreter]* We were very close. She could have stayed with us as much as she'd wanted—

the entire war. She knew she wasn't a big burden on us. It's war. It's hard, but we could have.

Narrator. That July, they spent most of their time indoors. It was the heaviest bombardment of the war so far. Thousands of shells fell daily. After a month, Bosko's mother couldn't take it any longer.

Mrs. Brkic. *[through interpreter]* I cannot choose any one moment—not the bread line massacre, not the shelling of my apartment—because everything was so tragic for me. When I saw that the town was completely destroyed, I just said, "Oh, my God. Is it possible that this can happen in this century?"

Narrator. In desperation, Rada turned to the only person she knew who could get her out of Sarajevo to join Bosko's older brother in Serbia. Her son, Bane, had grown up with a Muslim friend, a boy who was known as Celo.

Mrs. Brkic. *[through interpreter]* I've known him since he was 7 years old. He and Bane were in the same class and he liked Bane very much. He protected Bane in school. He was a strong kid. They talked the same language.

Celo. *[through interpreter]* Rada was like my mother. When my mother died, Rada helped me. Bane and I were always together, day and night. He'd go home and take a shower. I'd go home and take a shower. And then we'd be together again. And Bosko was like our younger brother. Sometimes we'd meet him and tell him to come with us.

Narrator. When Celo was 17, the tough Muslim was arrested for armed robbery and rape and sent to a maximum security prison. Inside Yugoslavia's Alcatraz, Celo made an important connection when he protected a frail political prisoner, Alia Izetbegovic, who would later become the president of Bosnia. After six years, Celo returned to the streets a hardened criminal, leading a gang that controlled much of Sarajevo's drug and protection rackets.

When Serbian attacks began, the 29-year-old gangster organized the first armed resistance to defend his city.

Celo. *[through interpreter]* Why did I do that? Let's just say that if somebody jumped on your head and started to pound you, wouldn't you defend yourself? And I wanted to defend myself and to defend my town.

Mr. Ismic. *[through interpreter]* But when this town was in the biggest danger, he came to defend this town. And because of that, for me, he is a good guy.

Mr. Cuk. *[through interpreter]* Celo was good to me and he was good to all Serbs on Koshevo Hill because he didn't let anybody touch them. Some people were coming and taking people away, but Celo saved many of us. You know, many Serbs stayed in Koshevo Hill.

Celo. *[through interpreter]* What's going on in Sarajevo is just survival. There was a duty for me to protect my town. It's not a war for heroes, like World War II. This is a civil war. In a civil war, you can't regard anybody as a hero. If I'm going to be a hero to Muslims, I don't want to be a hero. But if I'm a hero to all people in Sarajevo, no matter what nationality, I would be honored to be a hero.

Narrator. But Celo was quite prepared to play the hero, even posing for the part in a rock video. In real life, he had emerged as one of the most powerful people in the city. Between his military position and his criminal connections, he could get things done. Celo was the linchpin in exchanges of civilians and prisoners of war across the Muslim and Serb lines. Rada came to see her son's old friend at his headquarters.

Mrs. Brkic. *[through interpreter]* When we were alone, I said, "Celo, I want to leave Sarajevo," so he said he could fix that in the next three days. I asked him what we could do about Bosko and he said, "Bosko can stay. I will take care of him." So that was a big guarantee for me that Bosko would be all right.

Narrator. Getting out of the besieged city was dangerous. It meant taking one of the few routes out, and then only after arrangements had been made to hold fire. But there were no guarantees and people arrived on the other side shaken by the experience. Bosko's mother knew that it was a one-way trip.

Mrs. Brkic. *[through interpreter]* I said good-bye to everybody and then I told them only to take care about my Bosko. And then I specially said to Admira, "Take care of my Bosko," and she said, "I will."

Narrator. On August 23rd, 1992, during the heaviest shelling of the war, Bosko's mother and two other Serbs were smuggled out of Sarajevo in exchange for three Muslim prisoners of war.

By the summer of 1992, the Serb "ethnic cleansing" strategy was under way all over Bosnia. Muslims were rounded up in Nazi-like concentration camps or they were simply executed. The campaign claimed the lives of 200,000 Muslims, including six of Admira's relatives.

Mrs. Ismic. *[through interpreter]* Bosko was appalled, like everybody else. We didn't expect that from Serbs who lived with us. He couldn't understand how it could happen. He couldn't understand how people could do that to each other, Serbs killing Muslims. He couldn't understand the purpose and why and where such a crime came from, where such hatred came from.

Narrator. As the Serbs tightened their grip on Sarajevo, Bosko and Admira began to worry that a sudden shift in the front line could suddenly cut them off from each other. In September they decided to move in together in Bosko's old apartment on Koshevo Hill.

Mr. Cuk. *[through interpreter]* They had decided that they would never be separated again. Bosko said, "She's there with her parents and if they decided to divide the town in two, then I can't help her, and so it's better for us to be together. It doesn't matter what will happen."

Mrs. Ismic. *[through interpreter]* Especially for Bosko, it bothered him that they were not married because he had such respect for my husband, Zijo, so he was always worried about what Zijo was going to say and think because they were not married. He tried to get me to persuade Admira to marry him, but she refused, saying "Those mixed marriages in the war are always covered by the media."

> **Christianne Amanpour, CNN:** Muslims, Croats and Serbs come to the town hall to get married, exchanging vows—

Narrator. Mixed marriage ceremonies at Sarajevo's city hall had become international media events and propaganda tools for the Bosnian government, determined to show the world that Muslims and Serbs could still live together.

Mrs. Ismic. *[through interpreter]* Admira didn't like that. "I don't want to make such a big deal out of it," she said. And when I said, "Do it privately, just with the two of you and the best man" so nobody would know, and that's it, and then she told me, "I would feel so sorry to get married without anybody from Bosko's side of the family."

Narrator. Meanwhile, the war was taking a terrible toll on Admira's family. Her favorite cousin, Brana, the mother of two boys, had lost her husband before the war and then she was killed by a 60-millimeter shell while putting her sons to bed. The boys were so traumatized by witnessing their mother's death, they refused to leave the courtyard of their apartment building. Bosko and Admira soon became surrogate parents for the two orphans.

Goran. *[through interpreter]* I knew Bosko and Admira almost from the day I was born. They took me everywhere. Admira was here on my birthday.

Vanja. *[through interpreter]* She brought me books. The last time, she gave me three books. Before that, she gave me six. She was bringing me different books all the time. And she brought us chocolate that Bosko got from the army.

Mrs. Ismic. *[through interpreter]* Admira took toys to them. She knitted sweaters, made slippers for them— anything to make them happy. It's war. You're not able to buy anything—no stores. It's only what you can find on the black market, if somebody's selling something. It was hard to find anything, but they would constantly go there. They loved those kids so much.

Narrator. The first winter of the war hit Sarajevo hard. The city had been without power or running water for months. Its citizens were forced to make long, dangerous treks to the few public water supplies scattered throughout the city. Muslims, Croats and Serbs were drawn together by the daily struggle for survival.

On Koshevo Hill, Jurko Radojevic, a Serbian neighbor, relied on the young couple who lived downstairs.

Jurko Radojevic. *[through interpreter]* Bosko carried water to me all last winter. It was only rarely that he couldn't do it, but—nobody had electricity. They didn't have any and I didn't have any. We helped each other because I had an old wood stove, which I'd found in a burned-down house, and we baked bread in it together. We always shared every piece of bread.

Narrator. The winter was unusually harsh and across the city, a desperate population scrounged for fuel wherever it could be found. But the young man on Koshevo Hill remained generous.

Ms. Radojevic. *[through interpreter]* He never did anything bad to anybody. He was always coming with a kilo of flour or rice to try to help out, but he never came to your door to take something.

Narrator. A bag of rice or flour now cost a small fortune in a city where people were forced to use a bunch of weeds to stave off starvation for days. Sarajevo was now completely dependent on the United Nations relief flights for food and medicine. To supplement these meager rations, Sarajevans relied on the black market that flourished thanks to corrupt soldiers serving in UNPROFOR, the United Nations peace-keeping force. Coffee, cigarettes and gasoline stolen from UNPROFOR depots appeared on the black market at 10 or 20 times their original value.

Unable to operate his store any longer, Bosko, like many other Sarajevans, became an operator in the black market. Misa Cuk was his partner, but was reluctant to admit the extent of their illegal business.

Mr. Cuk. *[through interpreter]* You have to make money to live. It wasn't so much petrol, but coffee and things like that.

John Zaritsky *[through interpreter]* You can't tell me that it's not petrol and diesel.

Mr. Cuk. *[through interpreter]* Yes, it was that, too. It was a dirty job, but it was better with stuff like that. Celo told us we could do that.

Mr. Zaritsky. *[through interpreter]* Celo told us you were dealing in petrol and diesel the whole war.

Mr. Cuk. *[through interpreter]* Yes. Yes. Celo told us we could do that.

Celo. *[through interpreter]* Petrol. They were dealing in petrol with UNPROFOR. You know what a good business it is, dealing with UNPROFOR? You take one ton of petrol at night and sell it by next morning, so you're ahead 2,000 or 3,000 Deutschmarks, even more.

Mrs. Ismic. *[through interpreter]* Misa and Bosko were inseparable. He was with him all the time. He would come here and he was in their apartment all the time, also. Bosko felt badly for him. His mother was gone, his wife was gone and he was all alone, so he brought him home very often for lunch and he spent evenings in their place. So during this war, they were inseparable.

Narrator. In the spring of 1993, as the war entered its second year, Misa Cuk was a desperate man. In late April, he volunteered to drive Bosko and Admira from Koshevo Hill to a wedding in central Sarajevo. In a lavish ceremony, Celo was getting married. Generals, cabinet ministers, all of Sarajevo's elite was there. Bosko and Admira were honored to be invited. But as they celebrated, Misa Cuk was disappearing, fleeing out of Sarajevo, carrying with him a gun, a two-way radio and secret military codes from his unit in the Bosnian army. He had told Bosko nothing.

Mr. Ismic. *[through interpreter]* He put Bosko in a very grave situation. I would never do that to a friend. I don't know if he thought about that or how deep or strong that friendship was, but I could never do that to a friend. It's very unpleasant if you and I are friends and then you leave me here and go to the other side. This is war—people shooting, people dying. Misa should have thought about what would happen, but Misa didn't think anymore. It's terrible, Misa's mistake.

Narrator. Misa's mistake would cost Bosko and Admira dearly.

In April of 1993, the Western powers were debating whether air strikes or military intervention could bring a halt to the siege of Sarajevo. Misa was now with his wife and children in Serbia-controlled Bosnia while Bosko remained behind to face the consequences of his friend's desertion.

Celo. *[through interpreter]* So when Misa did that . . . — I mean, escaping—then the pressure on Bosko started. Some guys in our army started to attack him, even sometimes physically. One of them threw a rock at him, and so I had to protect him again. If I hadn't protected him, they would have killed him. He'd disappear.

Mr. Ismic. *[through interpreter]* The neighborhood reacted in a very ugly way because Misa had a reputation there as commander of Koshevo Hill and then the commander flees to the other side. So they had the urge to retaliate against somebody connected to Misa, but Misa had nobody there except them, so they turned against them because they were the people who spent time with Misa.

Ms. Radojevic. *[through interpreter]* They knew they weren't ever separated. They were together all winter.

And then, when they found out that Misa had escaped, they started to talk differently about Bosko.

Mr. Zaritsky. *[through interpreter]* Here in the neighborhood?

Ms. Radojevic. *[through interpreter]* Yes. Yes. They started to say that he was a Chetnik, that he should be in jail.

Narrator. Bosko was harassed daily by angry Muslim neighbors weary of the war and its hardships. One day in a bread line, when Bosko ended up with the last loaf, tempers flared.

Mrs. Ismic. *[through interpreter]* The people in the line didn't get any because there wasn't enough. And then one neighbor came out of the line and cursed the government and said, "How is it possible that a Chetnik can get bread and I cannot?" Bosko turned back and gave her their piece of bread—that's a little bit more than half a kilo—and then came back home. Admira was crying and he was in a bad mood.

Celo. *[through interpreter]* But he had to get out, one of those days, no matter how. He was in real danger because I couldn't be with him all the time. And you know how bad it is when your friend sells you out. Because Misa sold him out. It was classic.

Narrator. In early May, when Bosko received a summons ordering him to appear for questioning at a Muslim police station, he feared the worst. Serb traders were often tortured and killed in police custody. And 50 years earlier, during World War II, Bosko's grandfather had disappeared when he obeyed an order to report to the police.

Bosko had 72 hours to report or he would be arrested, and so he decided he must leave Sarajevo.

Sadika Ismic. *[through interpreter]* I was begging Bosko not to take Admira with him. "You go alone." I was begging both of them not to go. "How you lived until now you can live. If you want, you can live here in my place. Live in my place. Don't go there." And I'd ask him, "How can you take her there? You see what they are doing to the Muslim girls. You are helpless and they can do in front of your eyes what they want." They can kill her. They can slit her throat and everything else. "No, Grandma. The same way I spent so long here during the war and nobody has ever touched me, so nobody will touch her of mine."

Narrator. But Bosko and Admira had already decided they would leave Sarajevo together and escape to the Serbian side.

Mrs. Ismic. *[through interpreter]* I was so afraid. I knew terrible things were going on. Can you imagine how big that love is and the courage that she, as a Muslim, needed to go to the Serbian side, where all the Muslims were thrown out, where they take people to concentration camps, where they are raping, killing, where babies in carriages are killed? I couldn't understand how she had the courage to go.

Narrator. Bosko and Admira hid out at her grandmother's apartment until the gangster, Celo, could arrange their escape. When Bosko returned the next day to Koshevo Hill, he discovered their apartment had been looted by his neighbors.

Ms. Radojevic. *[through interpreter]* When he came back to his apartment, he called my son to see him, to say good-bye, but he didn't tell him that he was going to cross to the other side. My son said to him, "Take care, Bosko. You know how many friends you have, but you have even more enemies."

Narrator. On May 13th, Admira and her mother baked a cake to celebrate her 25th birthday.

Mrs. Ismic. *[through interpreter]* Bosko came back in the afternoon. He yelled from the door, "Do we have any cake?" "Yes, we have fruit cake," Admira said. Bosko sat at the table, took some cake and asked, "Where's the fruit?" We were all laughing. "Fruit will be next year," Admira said. So like that they celebrated her last birthday.

Narrator. On May 19th, the day they were to leave, Admira arrived early at her parents' house.

Mrs. Ismic. *[through interpreter]* Leaving her cat was very hard. Yellow was her darling. She asked me to take care of him, to pet him like she did. He slept with her in her room, so she said, "Mum, please sleep with him so he's not alone."

Narrator. That morning, Admira's mother made one final effort to persuade her daughter to stay.

Mrs. Ismic. *[through interpreter]* And Admira said, "Mum, do you know what you are asking from me? I can't do anything else but to go with him. Go back to the past, about 30 years ago. Would you have gone with Father?" I couldn't lie, even if it would have stopped her. I would have gone to the end of the world. But this is something different. This is a war. We couldn't convince her and she didn't want to talk about it.

Mr. Ismic. *[through interpreter]* I didn't say good-bye to either one. To either one, I didn't say good-bye. They planned their escape without me because I disagreed. They avoided saying good-bye to me.

Narrator. Back at her grandmother's apartment, Admira and Bosko packed their clothing and some jewelry from Bosko's family in two small suitcases.

Sadika Ismic. *[through interpreter]* She had sewn money into their clothes. I told them, "Hide your money. They can take your money and where can you go after that? You cannot buy food. You cannot pay for a bus." And she put 3,500 Deutschmark into her waistband and he put money in his pockets. I told him, "Bosko, how can you do that, just like that?" And he said, "No, nobody will do anything." He was 100 percent sure that everything would be more than good when he got to the other side. Before she got in the car, she waved to us, so they went like that. We stayed and cried. We waited for them to call—waited and waited. "I'll call you, Grandma, right away." But they never.

Narrator. On the Serbian side, two soldiers originally from Koshevo Hill, and old friends of Bosko and Celo, had negotiated with the gangster for the couple's escape. Sasa Bogdanovic had done many deals with Celo during the war and Milkan Gaborovic had been trying to get his relatives out of the besieged city.

Milkan Gaborovic. *[through interpreter]* I was waiting for Celo's call and he called me and said, "Look, I'll send you Bosko and Admira now and tomorrow at the same time, your aunt and cousin." I told him, "Give me my aunt and cousin first, and then Bosko and Admira." He said that Bosko had problems, that he'd gotten a call from the police and he must send them now.

Sasa Bogdanovic. *[through interpreter]* Milkan had asked me to help him because I had worked on exchanges before. He had set up everything on all front lines so that no one would open fire. That was the only condition which Celo would let them leave.

Narrator. Late in the afternoon, Admira and Bosko arrived at Celo's headquarters in Sarajevo.

Celo. *[through interpreter]* Bosko was a little nervous. Admira wasn't. I got it set up with our men, but I told him, "Wait until dark." There it's no-man's land, surrounded by four or five different forces—Shatzo's police, special police units, HVO and Chetniks—and it's impossible to make a deal with all of them.

Dino Kapin. *[through interpreter]* We didn't know at all that somebody was supposed to cross. That zone is prohibited from any kind of movement.

Narrator. Dino Kapin was a commander of a Croatian unit allied with the Muslim army on the Sarajevo side of the front line. He had a rooftop view of the no-man's land where Admira and Bosko would try to cross.

Mr. Kapin. *[through interpreter]* This—I was on the front line on May 19th. It was a nice day. About 5:00 o'clock in the afternoon, from the direction of our checkpoint, a man and a woman were walking with some bags towards their lines.

Mr. Bogdanovic. *[through interpreter]* I was calling to Bosko and whistled at him and he whistled back. That was the only way I could get him to notice me because I was down low and there was no way for me to show my face, nor could I wave at him, or I could be seen myself and get shot. Anyway, it was about—they were about 15 or 20 yards away.

Mrs. Ismic. *[through interpreter]* I found a letter she had left with cat food. She hadn't told me she had written me a letter.

2nd Reader. "My dear Mum: It seems we are finally leaving tonight and whatever happens is God's will. I'll call you as soon as we are safely on the other side. I most worry about you and my little Yellow. Bosko and I have been talking about when the war is over, we will come back to Sarajevo. Everything will be fine, like the war never happened. Do not worry about me. Think about yourself. It will be much easier for me. I love you so much. Your Admira."

Mr. Bogdanovic. *[through interpreter]* So they were walking and skipping. And when they came to the intersection, we heard one bullet. It was a sniper's bullet that landed in front of their legs.

Mr. Kapin. *[through interpreter]* Just after they passed Vrbanja Bridge, Chetniks opened fire at them. The guy, as far as I could tell, was killed instantly and the girl was injured. She was screaming and started to crawl over to him. And then she hugged him. And then there was no sign of life.

Mr. Bogdanovic. *[through interpreter]* In the first instants, I didn't believe it. I didn't believe that they were dead, that they were shot, even that it was them. I thought maybe somebody else got shot. I couldn't believe it because I thought what Celo organized was always a strong and safe connection.

Celo. *[through interpreter]* It's very hard for me to talk about it. I loved them very much. I felt badly he didn't listen to me.

Narrator. That night in Serbia, Misa Cuk heard the news.

Mr. Cuk. *[through interpreter]* I said, "I will come right now to Sarajevo." I couldn't believe it. I couldn't believe he was killed. So I went to the Serbian side of Sarajevo and I saw how they were lying there.

Narrator. Two days later, the bodies of Admira and Bosko still lay where they had fallen.

Mrs. Ismic. *[through interpreter]* At about 11:00

o'clock, the phone rang. I picked it up and it was a ham radio operator from Serbia. He asked me to confirm information that he had received that Admira and Bosko were killed on a bridge in Sarajevo. I was thunderstruck. It was a terrible shock.

Narrator. Admira's mother, not believing the news, went to Celo's headquarters, where he told her what happened.

Mrs. Ismic. *[through interpreter]* Bosko died instantly. Admira was alive for five or ten minutes. She was injured, but crawled over to him and hugged him and then didn't move anymore. So they died together like that. After that, I was tortured with the worry—"Oh, my God. Did she feel any pain? Did she feel any fear? Was she aware that she was going to die?" She probably saw that Bosko was dead because as she crawled over, she was conscious. Terrible. I will never know that and I am so tortured with that.

Mrs. Brkic. *[through interpreter]* They died for each other. I mean, even now, I can see them hugging each other in my mind.

Mr. Ismic. *[through interpreter]* I still don't believe that they're dead because it's very hard to believe such young people like that can disappear with such a sudden and violent death. All their wishes, all plans are sunk after one bullet, after one burst, after one move, after one monstrous act. That's the proof that love cannot conquer all. Love cannot win over people who don't believe in love. But these people who are shooting at us don't believe in love. For them, love doesn't exist. All their love and hatred they show through cannons, machine guns, pistols and guns. And so that's their love. Their love is a bullet and nothing more.

Television Anchor. In the Bosnian capital, Sarajevo, Serb rebels and the Muslim-led authorities have spent the day arguing over which side has claim to the bodies of a young couple who were shot dead and left lying in no-man's land. They were both 25—he a Serb and she a Muslim.

Narrator. As the days passed, Serb and Muslim authorities continued to accuse each other of shooting Bosko and Admira.

Mr. Kapin. *[through interpreter]* There doesn't exist any possibility that the shooting came from this side because the position of the bodies would be absolutely different. When we were watching, the bullets came towards us because we were watching each other face to face. It couldn't be any other way.

Mr. Bogdanovic. *[through interpreter]* I've been 18 months in the war and I'm a soldier. I'm a fighter. So I can judge from which side fire came and from where. So I'm more than sure. From our side, nobody has any reason to shoot them because they were coming to us alive.

Celo. *[through interpreter]* During our investigation into which side she was facing—she tried to cover herself with her jacket from the side where the bullets came from. She crawled to him and covered her face from the side where the bullets came from. And on the pictures you can see which side she's facing. She wasn't facing our side.

Mr. Gaborovic. *[through interpreter]* After it happened, I talked to Celo and I asked him, "Celo, how could you do this to me?" And then he asked me, "How can you do this to me?" And I swore at him and he said he'd kill my cousin and aunt and I told him, "You can do that, but I'll do the same to your family."

Narrator. But there was one thing the enemies could agree on: There was no motive, no logic, no reason.

Celo. *[through interpreter]* There was no specific reason. It was just butchery, like somebody came into view in a neutral zone and then—I don't know. They don't know. None of the soldiers know. Somebody said, "Let me open fire. . . ." It's as simple as that.

Mr. Bogdanovic. *[through interpreter]* This is a big front line of Muslims and Serbians and there are so many mentally sick people who carry a gun. They are everywhere. You never know which fool will start to shoot to kill when they see somebody.

Mr. Gaborovic. *[through interpreter]* Their bags disappeared two nights before we rescued the bodies. They snuck up close and grabbed the bags with hooks, probably because they thought there would be big money. They were saying around town that they had about 100,000 Deutschmark. Because I was there every night, I saw their bodies being hit with Molotov cocktails and they were shooting incendiary bullets to try to burn them, but they didn't succeed.

Narrator. Once again, the Serbs and Muslims blamed each other for trying to destroy the bodies, which would have eliminated any evidence of which side had fired the fatal bullets.

Mrs. Ismic. *[through interpreter]* I thought we were going to go crazy. For days they lay on the street. That was May and it was very hot for Sarajevo. On the streets roved hungry dogs and cats, but they were in the middle of downtown. That's just 250 yards from the Holiday Inn. In the heat, on the street, and we're not able to do anything. We tried through our army, through the presidency, through UNPROFOR. We thought UNPROFOR was going to help us. Everybody told us UNPROFOR was there for humanitarian reasons. "They must do that because they are paid to do that." Foreign journalists, especially Reuters, told us that. But UNPROFOR didn't do anything, even when I came to talk to them. They wouldn't even let me in.

Narrator. Admira's father told the U.N. forces he would retrieve the bodies himself if they gave him an armored personnel carrier.

Mr. Ismic. *[through interpreter]* I told them that none of their men needed to take the risk of getting the bodies. I would do that alone. "I will get the bodies into the APC." But they turned me down. They were so uninterested that it looked like we're here because of UNPROFOR and not because UNPROFOR is here for us.

> **Television Reporter.** It took a week before Serb militiamen retrieved their bodies, because the area was so dangerous. But mystery surrounds the deaths.

Narrator. The Serbs claimed a team of their commandos rescued the bodies during the night.

> **Serbian Military Spokesman.** *[subtitles]* We rescued the bodies mainly for humanitarian reasons, and to show the other side that we are not the monsters they accuse us of being.

Narrator. Only later would the truth be revealed.

Mr. Bogdanovic. *[through interpreter]* The bodies were rescued by a Muslim crew. They tied ropes around them and pulled them out.

Narrator. In a cruel irony, the Serbs won their propaganda victory by sending Muslim prisoners to rescue the bodies and to risk being shot by their comrades in Sarajevo.

Mr. Bogdanovic. *[through interpreter]* They couldn't know at the moment, in the dark, that there were Muslims that were coming to get the bodies. When you are in the dark, you just hear a noise so you just open fire at the place where you hear the noise. And there was really a possibility that those Muslims who went out could be killed.

Narrator. The bodies were moved to a Serbian military morgue. No autopsies were performed and so there were no final answers as to who fired the shots.

Mrs. Brkic. *[through interpreter]* When I went to the morgue and asked the man in charge if he had any more information about them, he said, "No, I don't have anything about them. But for everybody that is brought in here, I have a paper with at least a name." They were just in the book under the numbers 250 and 251. And I signed for them in that book. Just those two numbers. Nothing else.

Narrator. Both families wanted their children returned to Sarajevo, but the Serbs said no, and so they were buried in a bleak military cemetery as part of a service for a Serb soldier. Father Charkich, the Serb military chaplain who had known Admira's father in Sarajevo, officiated.

Father Charkich. *[through interpreter]* Since she is a Muslim and he is a Serb, there was a question about the funeral until an understanding was reached with certain people. We came to an agreement that they'd be buried next to each other. Since she's a Muslim, I did not conduct prayers for her, but she was beside Bosko at the same time prayers were said.

Narrator. At the end, Bosko's mother presented a final gift, a sweater she had knit for Admira.

Narrator. The Serbs had offered safe passage to Admira's parents to attend the funeral, but they refused to participate in what they saw as more Serb propaganda.

Mrs. Brkic. *[through interpreter]* My dearest kids, rest in peace. Your destiny is to be together in the grave.

Narrator. Zijo watched the ceremony on T.V.

Mr. Ismic. *[through interpreter]* Even their henchmen buried them together. Even they couldn't show disrespect for their love. It doesn't matter if they were their executioners. They still couldn't separate them. Probably that is destiny.

Mrs. Ismic. *[through interpreter]* All the time I thought if I could only go to the grave to give flowers, to see how it looked—but there isn't any possibility for that. It was terrible for me, on August 11—because that was Bosko's birthday. He would have been 25 years old. I cried all day. On that day, we wrote a letter to Rada. I wish so much I could go to his grave and place 25 roses for 25 years. For us, it is still impossible. We are hoping that something will change and that the madness will stop, that we will bring our kids to our town. There must be an end to all of this. I don't know how long it will take, but some day it has to stop.

Mrs. Brkic. *[through interpreter]* I will never go back to Sarajevo. I will never go because of the two of them, even if there was a castle waiting for me there. I couldn't go through the same streets which they had walked. I couldn't go into that apartment anymore. I could never go into that apartment again. Never.

Narrator. In Sarajevo, the spring rains have come again. It's been almost a year.

Mrs. Ismic. *[through interpreter]* I still cannot accept the reality that the two of them are gone. They promised that they would come back. When I saw Admira off, I said, "Mama will count the days until you return," and I am still counting the days, one by one, but I know there will be no end.

Mr. Ismic. *[through interpreter]* The rest of my life I will spend bringing Bosko and Admira's murderers to trial, to be punished like they deserve. I will always try to do that. If I can't do it that way, I will choose my way and my way is an eye for an eye and a head for a head.

Narrator. After 22 months of bombardment and 10,000 deaths in Sarajevo, the West threatened air strikes and the Serb forces withdrew. An uneasy peace finally settled on the city. "A glooming peace this morning with it brings / The sun for sorrow will not show his head / Go hence to have more talk of these sad things / Some shall be pardoned and some punished / Where never was a story of more woe than this of Juliet and her Romeo."